CALLIOPE

2012: THE 19TH ANTHOLOGY OF WOMEN WHO WRITE

Featuring the winners of the International Short Prose and Poetry Contest

Calliope 2012: the 19th Anthology
By Women Who Write, Inc.

Published annually by

Women Who Write, Inc.
P.O. Box 6167
Louisville, KY 40206-0167

ISBN 978-0-9883673-0-2

Library of Congress Control Number: 2012918366

Cover design:
Shellee Marie Jones at www.shellee.com

To order or for more information, see www.womenwhowrite.com. For bulk orders or to schedule a reading, please contact info@womenwhowrite.com.

"Thou, Calliope, queen of the groves of song, uplift thy lyre and begin the tale."

—Thebaid 4.32

In Greek mythology, Calliope was the oldest of the nine daughters of Zeus, king of the gods, and Mnemosyne, goddess of memory. The daughters were collectively known as the nine muses; each daughter was assigned a specific literary or artistic dimension.

Calliope was the muse of epic poetry and eloquence or prose. She is often pictured holding a writing tablet and stylus, sometimes with a book or scroll, and wearing a gold crown. She inspired Homer to write the "Iliad" and the "Odyssey."

Ancient Greek writers and artists believed that any of the muses could be called upon for help, regardless of their assigned responsibility. They regularly asked their favorite muse for inspiration.

Today, a muse can be anything that inspires the flow of creative energy—meditation, a special room or place, or music.

Literature abounds with artists' accounts of relationships—real and imaginary—with their muses.

The members of Women Who Write dedicate our annual anthology to women readers and writers, and to those who love them. We share the joy and productivity of those who have found their muse, and support and encourage those who still struggle in their search.

Dedicated to all women who aspire to express themselves through the written word; we are kindred spirits.

Contributing Member Authors

Emily Boone
Cynthia Clegg Canada
J. Watson Finger
Margaret F. (Peggy) Grimes
Carroll Grossman
Susan E. Lindsey
Mariam Williams

Table of Contents

Third Place Prose

Honorable Mention: Poetry

Honorable Mention Prose

Member Submissions

About Women Who Write, Inc.

Women Who Write, Inc. is an organization of women writers who are dedicated to excellence in literary creation. Our mission is to welcome, encourage, educate, and support women who aspire to write. All women interested in writing, at any level, in any genre, amateur or professional, are invited to join.

The organization meets the first Thursday of each month at 6:30 p.m. at the Highlands Branch of the Louisville Free Public Library, located at 1250 Bardstown Road in the Mid-City Mall, Louisville, Kentucky. If you are looking for support, encouragement, and valuable feedback on your writing, please join us.

Annual membership dues are $50 and entitle members to participate in monthly meetings (which include readings and critiques), writing-related workshops and training, guest lectures, publication in our annual anthology, and participation in our annual retreat.

Women Who Write is a 501(c)(3) non-profit organization. Donations are gratefully accepted to support our mission and are tax-deductible.

Please visit our website, www.womenwhowrite.com, for more information.

About the International Short Prose and Poetry Contest

The 2012 *Calliope* is the 19th annual anthology published by Women Who Write. The book showcases the work of the winners of our International Short Prose and Poetry Contest, as well as the work of our members.

The contest is open to all women writers over the age of eighteen. In 2012, we received 135 entries from women in thirty states and five countries. Winners were chosen in a blind judging by independent judges.

Our 2012 prose judges were Annette Allen and Molly McCaffrey; our 2012 poetry judge was Kathleen Driskell. We extend our special thanks to them for careful consideration of all the entries. Their biographies are included elsewhere in this book.

The winning entries in the poetry and prose categories are included in *Calliope,* in addition to works written by Women Who Write members. Our members are not eligible to win in either category, but *Calliope* offers them the opportunity to be published. For many, this is the first time their work has been published.

Some of the content in this anthology addresses adult themes and may include language that is offensive to some people. The anthology is intended for adult readers.

We hope that you enjoy these poems, stories, and essays. Please watch our website, www.womenwhowrite.com, for information on the 2013 International Short Prose and Poetry Contest.

Poetry Judge

Kathleen Driskell was the poetry judge for the 2012 International Short Prose and Poetry Contest. Her book of poems, *Seed Across Snow,* was listed as a national bestseller by the Poetry Foundation. Her most recent publication is *Peck and Pock: A Graphic Poem.* Her poems have appeared in many nationally known literary journals including *Poems and Plays*, the *Southern Review,* and *Rattle*. Driskell is an Al Smith Fellow of the Kentucky Arts Council. She teaches creative writing and helps direct the brief-residency MFA in Writing Program at Spalding University in Louisville.

Prose Judges

Annette Allen is professor of humanities at the University of Louisville and director of the humanities doctoral program in China. She has published two collections of poetry, *Country of Light* (1996) and *What Vanishes* (2006), and she is the recipient of three state arts council awards for poetry, and two NEH summer fellowships. She has published essays on poets Mary Oliver and Sylvia Plath, as well as writer Virginia Woolf. Her latest publication is a co-edited book, *Clinical Ethics and the Necessity of Stories,* in the philosophy and medicine series, which stems from her new interest in narrative medicine. A MacDowell Colony Fellow and a Kentucky Arts Council Poetry Fellowship winner, Allen continues to publish her poetry in journals and small presses while working on her next collection.

Molly McCaffrey is the author of the short story collection, *How to Survive Graduate School & Other Disasters*, the co-editor of the short fiction anthology, *Commutability: Stories about the Journey from Here to There*, and the founder of *I Will Not Diet*, a blog devoted to healthy living and body acceptance. Nominated for three Pushcart Prizes, an AWP Intro Journals Award, and Scribner's Best of the Fiction Workshops, she received her Ph.D. from the University of Cincinnati, and currently teaches at Western Kentucky University in Bowling Green, Kentucky. She is at work on her first memoir, *You Belong to Us*, which tells the story of when she met her biological family.

Winners of the 2012 International Short Prose and Poetry Contest

First Place

Poetry: Eileen Malone, *Just a Boat*

Prose: Caitlin O'Neil, *Waitress*

Second Place

Poetry: Katie Caswell, *A Lesson from Picasso: Portrait of War*

Prose: Rachael Peckham, *Digging Myself a Little Hole*

Third Place

Poetry: Andrea Bates, *As If We Were Ancient Egyptians*

Prose: Jamie Hoey, *Spider Webs*

Honorable Mention

Poetry: Lakshmi Narayanan, *Aging August Rainfall*

Prose: Marina Petrova, *The Pharmacy*

Just a Boat

By Eileen Malone

There used to be days
the overturned rowboat
rotting away at the edge of the lake
appeared as the skeleton
of a huge cryptid, bleached to alabaster

then nights the wrecked boat
looked more a giant moon-stoned jewel
on the brocade bank of the oil-black lake

but now, as they say, just like that
it has come to this: the boat is just a boat
and I don't miss him anymore

my loss of him that for years
has sliced into and cut open my life
has been replaced with the ghost
of a rowboat that edges over glassy waters
its oars trolling, trawling for a new space
casting about to hold something
anything that indicates the presence
of his absence.

Waitress

By Caitlin O'Neil

By ten o'clock Saturday night, Ray and I are the only staffers left at The Cap'n Jack. We stand in the stark fluorescent light of the galley kitchen, looking through garlands of fishing net into the darkened restaurant, where Kath sits, smoking a cigarette, and counting the day's receipts as her father watches from the giant sign in the driveway. The teak tables have been wiped down and covered in sailcloth. The squat ketchup bottles have been married so they will remain eternally full. The knotted rope coasters are stacked on the bar, and Kath has locked away top-shelf liquors to prevent underage waitresses from supplementing our tips. I don't earn as much as the other girls, so each time Kath hands me the slim stack of bills, it feels like the final tally of my failure.

I have graduated from my father's A-list private college and was supposed to get a real job, but there are no real jobs. So I am waiting tables, which everyone tries to pretend is quaint and down-to-earth after a $200,000 education, but which in reality is depressing and a bit scary. I can't even manage to turn this waitressing job into something more, the way my mother did, though you're not supposed to hope your daughter will marry rich any more. Or you're not supposed to talk about it. Either way, I'm already rich, so there's nothing left to hope for. Instead, I am saving for a car that I will drive away from these disappointments into a future I can't picture yet.

Kath tells me I am a bad fit with the rest of the staff, but she keeps me on because of my mother, who worked here every summer of her college career. They are one big, happy family, returning to the Cape year after year with such unwavering loyalty that I wonder if Kath has laced their virgin daiquiris so they see the place the way it was when Kath's dad opened it, sleek and modern and new. They don't see what I see: a run-down seaside restaurant serving flash-frozen fish from Canada to droves of happily duped tourists who have come to celebrate some bygone idea of summer. They're so deluded it almost cheers me up.

I start making clams casino, wrapping the slippery iodine bodies in strips of congealing bacon while Ray sprays down the last of the cooking pots. The ancient chrome washer blows off steam in great gauzy cascades as dishes rotate through its caustic stomach. We've turned up the radio on the windowsill so we can hear the baseball game over the mechanical roar. Papelbon, the closer, has just entered the game for the Red Sox. The first two batters strike out swinging.

"Five bucks says he gets the next guy," shouts Ray. He is pre-med at U Mass Dartmouth. Each summer he works three jobs to make up for the money he loses when he's in school. He starts each morning with a shift at his parents' convenience store, spends his day landscaping, and ends here in the kitchen with me. I envy his work ethic, his certainty about where it all will lead. This job is my first ever, and it's all I can do to keep from getting fired.

"Who's the next guy?"

"Who cares?" He mops his face with the hem of his tank top, revealing a soft, fleshy stomach the color of caramel. "Take a chance."

"I can't bet if I don't know who he's up against."

"Now or never. Five bucks." Ray shoots me with the water gun until the front of my shorts is soaked.

"Five bucks!" I cry and chuck a raw clam at him. It hits the wall behind him and slides down, leaving a slimy white trail.

"Whoever he is, I hope he throws better than you do."

Ray drops his water gun, I wipe my hands on my despised Welcome Aboard apron, and together we listen to the announcer call the at-bat. I think I can hear the ball hit the glove each time, though it is likely just static. Papelbon strikes out the last batter.

"Game over." Ray does a victory lap around the dishwasher, circling back to pluck five soft, wrinkled bills—money I had plans for, money I can't afford to lose—from my fingers. Even though he's been working since six a.m., Ray is helpful, fun, and easygoing. Kath doesn't hate Ray the way she hates me.

When the clams are chilling in the walk-in freezer and the pots are hanging from their hooks over the stove, Ray and I pull the door out behind us and walk across the street to the beach. We sit on the rotting wooden stairs and smoke the joint I've stolen from the cigar box under my brother's bed. With our lungs full of smoke, we look out across the water to the rambling beach houses crowning the opposite shore. They look ancient and knowing, with their weathered shingles and fresh white trim. I wonder if Kath looks out on these houses and thinks of my mother, who married into such wealth from the same humble beginnings.

My parents had met, of course, at The Cap'n Jack.

My father—his lean frame freed of its blue banker's suit, his skin browned and salted from a day on the water—dined on sole. My mother, ever confident, noted his sea-worthiness and asked for a sail. She didn't figure that their journey would end across the river in his family's big old house. But it did, and as a result, I have spent my childhood summers looking staring down at The Cap'n Jack, waiting for my turn to show my mother that I am every bit the girl she was. Only it turns out I am not.

Ray kisses the side of my head and lets his mouth linger there, his lips warm from the smoke.

"No one should own a beach," I tell him. The ocean comes and goes, lapping at the edge of the stairs and spraying foam up onto our legs.

"Easy for you to say. Beach owner." Ray runs his hand along my salty thigh.

"Don't you think there's something sad about it?" I gesture to the hard-packed sand studded with glistening shells. "It's like countries claiming airspace or farming the ocean."

"I think the people with beaches are the only ones who worry about it." Ray moves his arms up my waist and pulls me close. "If it's so wrong, why don't you do something?"

It's the question I've been asking myself all summer as I contemplate my title: waitress. The girl who waits. For what? I wonder. But now that the usual avenues are blocked—no entry-level consultancy or PR post for me; even my father's silver-spoon bank is botched—I can only drive and hope the future comes into view.

"You are all talk, no action." Ray smiles slyly, smoke leaking out the corners of his mouth.

He lays out the dare and I kiss him with an open mouth. Before he can unhook my bra, I slide my hands up his shirt and run them over his stone-smooth skin, feeling his body give in gentle puckers at my touch. Most girls won't tell you that they like softness in a man. But I do. We are all vulnerable underneath our hard shells.

When I arrive at four the following afternoon, an hour before we open for the last night of the summer, Kath is on the warpath.

"Who forgot to prep the salads?" she shouts.

Kath knows it is me, it is always me, but she likes to put on this show for the other waitresses—tan, pony-tailed girls smelling of coconut oil, who are still wearing their bikinis underneath their uniforms. I get bored at the beach so I ride my bike along the rail trail from Chatham to Wellfleet, which leaves my back red and my stomach pale, like a crab.

"It was me."

I leave the table where we are folding the napkins. Mine are always the most beautiful, knife-pleated and jaunty, while the other girls' slouch and sag. But that's not the sort of thing that counts with Kath.

I try to pass through the swinging door into the prep kitchen, but Kath blocks my way. She is short but wide, a human Jersey barrier.

"Last chance." She growls in my ear. "I need one more big weekend and I won't have you ruining it."

Our faces are so close that I could kiss her. I almost want to, to see what she would do. She is actually quite pretty—with her natural blonde hair pulled back in a knot to showcase her heart-shaped face and blue nickel eyes—but I can't get past her personality. I'll leave it to someone else to try to love her.

"It was so late," I explain. "The clams took forever."

"Ray managed to get everything done."

That's because the girls help him, I want to say, so he'll buy them beer. Which he hasn't since we started dating, another strike against me. But Kath would think it is only right that I am left to chop salad for four hundred, while Bart, the bartender, makes *real* strawberry daiquiris for the other girls, yet another storied Cap'n Jack tradition.

I flee to the walk-in freezer and fill my arms with purple-skinned onions and iceberg lettuce. I let them roll across the aluminum prep counter, thundering like bowling balls. Ray sticks his head in from the main kitchen.

"Need help?" He wears his Sox cap backwards. His dark curls stick to his forehead like seaweed.

I wave him off. "Don't even think about it."

The last thing I need is Kath coming in here to find Ray doing my job.

Ray strokes the back of my neck, like I'm a dog that needs soothing. "You've got to learn to roll with it, baby. Not everyone is going to love you."

"They all love you." With a cleaver, I cut the iceberg heads in half, again and again, until the lettuce is shredded in limp, watery strands.

"They don't know me. They love the idea of me. Hardworking brother."

"Well, they hate the idea of me." I whack the onions into lacey circles of uneven width. The smell pinches my nose and sets my eyes to watering. I pause to wipe my eyes.

Through the rigging, I can see Kath and the girls dancing around the room with their curvy pink glasses held high. Towering, balding Bart, in his gold-braided captain's hat and Jimmy Buffett T-shirt, turns up the Beach Boys "Fun, Fun, Fun" and strums his air guitar. It is just as my mother had described. For the millionth time, I wish I could be more like her—easygoing, able to fit in with the crowd. Then I would be out there with the other girls, rallying around Kath like lost members of her tribe. Instead, I stand watching from the kitchen, wishing they would trip and spill their drinks. Even Ray, whispering late-night plans in my ear, can't keep me from feeling left out.

"You forgot this." He holds up the half-smoked joint.

"Save it for me. I'm going to need it." I push his hand closed, fingers over palm like a clamshell. Then I turn and kiss Ray there in the kitchen. With my eyes closed, I can hear the fluorescent light buzzing overhead and the faint pull of the ocean in the distance. Maybe he is consolation enough.

The music stops. The door swings open. I should have known better.

"Stop kissing and clean up! Get out there! We have customers!"

Kath is red-faced and fuming, holding a bouquet of empty daiquiri glasses before her like a drunken bride.

"Get that dishwasher going. These glasses need to be clean. Salads! More salads!"

Ray and I watch her careen around the kitchen like an untied balloon losing its air. She throws the glasses into the sink and, miraculously, none of them break. Kath ties on an apron and starts washing out the pink foam herself, then stops and runs into the walk-in freezer.

"Clams casino! For everyone! On the house!"

She is about serve them cold when Perry, the been-there-done-that grill cook, emerges from behind the heat lamps and pulls the tray into the oven. "Let's cook 'em first, shall we?"

This comment knocks Kath back to earth. Ray pours her a glass of water.

"What's that?" Kath points at a piece of napkin caught in the plastic floor mats that I am supposed to roll up and mop underneath each night.

"It was only the salads I forgot. I did the floors, I swear." But then I realize the napkin is our joint.

"What the hell?" Kath picks up the joint and pockets it. Then she turns to me. "I would fire you right now, but I don't have time for this shit. All I'm asking for is one good night. Is that too much to ask?"

"Why do you assume it's mine?"

"You're going to try to tell me this belongs to him?" Kath tosses her head back and laughs. "I can't believe you're Kitty's girl. Do you realize your mother holds the record for most consecutive summers?"

"That was thirty years ago. Who cares?"

Kath flinches as if I've struck her. She cares, of course. If The Cap'n Jack is one episode in my mother's charmed life, it is Kath's whole existence. She looks at me—long limbs, prim nose, dark ponytail curled against my neck like a question mark—and sees my mother. Somehow Kath is still waiting for her charm, her candor, her ready smile, her we're-all-in-this-together gusto. She is again disappointed.

"I hope you're a little nicer to the customers than you are to me." Kath smoothes her bun and pinches her cheeks until they turn pink, readying herself for her return to the dining room.

"They make it easier."

"Where is it written it should be easy?" she says, then yells into the kitchen. "Perry? How are those clams?"

Perry slides a plate of clams under the heat lamps. Kath garnishes the frothy, bubbling shells with lemon and loads them onto a tray. She disappears through the door to the dining room, which will swing back and forth in a steady rhythm throughout the night as we serve up the summer's last suppers to the tourists filling the dining room. They savor the sweet corn on the cob, order the whole lobster instead of the tail, and save room for ice cream because this night will have to last all winter.

Later that night, Ray and I are alone in the kitchen again, closing up. Out front in the restaurant, Kath smokes the last of our joint and counts out the till. I can tell by her face that the news is not good.

"It's not your fault." Ray has left the dishwasher unattended and stands behind me, pressing his warm stomach into the small of my back. He smells of beer batter and lemon. I know he is smiling, but he isn't making me feel any better. "The world is changing."

"I know," I say. "But I don't understand how."

I feel like a bad omen, a bellwether of Kath's misfortune. If she can't befriend Kitty's girl, the end must be near. I wonder for the millionth time if there was a way I could have made myself fit in.

The dishwasher emits an angry hiss. Ray squeezes my elbow and leaves me to watch Kath smile ruefully as she pulls the stack of worn bills and receipts through her fingers again and again, stopping now and then for a drag from the joint, losing count and starting again.

After a while, she waves me over. She looks up, droopy-eyed and mellow. She hands me a short stack of bills, my last tips of the summer.

"You're a good kid, but a horrible waitress."

The finality of our exchange makes me reckless.

"You're a terrible boss."

"Maybe." She looks out the window, at the smiling sign in the driveway. "My dad was better at it. When he opened this place, there was nothing like it this far north. Dinner, dancing, ocean views. Like something out of a movie. Dean Martin came one night and asked for him by name." She turned toward the door, as if Dino might walk in now and save us all from the glamourless tedium that was our lives. Kath started as if she'd briefly dozed. "It's changed, of course, but people still love this place."

"They love the idea of this place."

"So? That counts for something. Isn't that why you're here?"

Of course, she's right. I'm here, just like she is, long after the others have gone, chasing ghosts, searching for a place that probably never existed.

"Your mother was amazing." Kath's bloodshot eyes flicker with light, and I wonder if she wasn't a little in love with her, just like everyone else.

"Don't remind me."

She reaches for the joint and is about to lift it to her lips when she changes her mind and offers it to me. I take it and inhale, and for the first time all summer, I'm doing something without picturing my mother doing it better. As I exhale, I realize this is how I will invent myself, not from my mother's memory or my father's money, but out of smoke, out of thin air. I am overcome with a feeling of gratitude and love for her and her stupid restaurant. So I tell her what she wants to hear.

"This restaurant is legendary. People will remember it."

Kath shines me one of the seesaw grins her father still mugs out the window behind her. I've finally said something right.

"They will, won't they?"

I nod. All we want is to be remembered, the way her dad is, the way my mother is, like the Cap'n Jack itself.

But we won't be.

There will be no next summer. After thirty-five years, Kath will be forced to close. Tonight, she will drop the cash at the bank with hope in her heart, but come next June, the windows will be boarded up, the sign covered with plastic. Customers looking to relive their summer memories will have to look elsewhere.

By then, I'll be the proud owner of a 1999 Honda Accord, which will break down three times on the way to New Mexico, where I'll relive my summer, waiting tables for another six months at a cowboy dive before I land a job leading bike trips through the pit of the Grand Canyon, hoping my life will be waiting on the other side. I spend my days capped by a hard red helmet. At night, I read emails from Ray laced with anatomical descriptions of what he'd like to do to me, if we had time or were in the same place.

But tonight the air is cool as I mop the floor and listen to the ballgame while Ray dries the pots. The Red Sox are losing; there is no game to save. When Ray is done, we turn out the lights and walk across the street. I can smell burnt pinesap from the hasty bonfires the summer people have lit on the town beach. Instead of joining them, we sit on the split-rail fence and stare back at the Cap'n Jack wondering how, or if, we'll remember it. I look over at Ray and wonder if we'll be telling the story of this summer to each other for the rest of our lives. I don't think so, but it's too soon to tell.

A Lesson from Picasso: Portrait of War

By Katie Caswell

Facing the Spanish artwork
Our American tour group stands in a grand room
Of the Reina Sophia Museum
Transfixed:
Our sighs truss together to create a collective wince.

The canvas speaks to our party in black and white—
Violence stirs in the grays, shadows of helplessness,
Of desperation.
War.

Picasso's *Guernica*
Devours our souls
With its sharp-edged tongues,
Like nails in a wooden coffin,
The canvas conjures missiles in our minds, raging.
Discordant images plead:
A mother's twisted tears fall on her naked infant.
A distorted grimace shouts in shame.
Wretched spirits girded with barbed wire struggle against savagery.

In this world, not one bird sings nor flower blooms—
Yesterday's false promises fade like a whisper.
The painting tells how
Hope has been dismembered.

There on the wall in black and white oil
A siren screams
In a broken sword
In broken souls
In perfidy.
Un beso de sangre en silencio . . .
De la boca del Toro.
A silent bloody kiss . . .
From the Bull's mouth.
Is this the lesson we will learn?

We look on.
A moment passes.
Lifetimes pass.
A tired tour guide speaks and
The spell is broken.
Helplessly, we shuffle on to the next painting.

Later, the white afternoon sunlight blinds us
When we exit the Reina Sophia.
Stepping out on the black stones of the cobbled plaza,
We hear the toll of a nearby cathedral's bell.
A resonant warning that it is getting late
Echoes through the medieval courtyards.

As we walk away from the museum and the violence of that canvas,
Our dark shadows—and *Guernica*'s—
Follow us
Onto the gray pavement of Madrid and
Everywhere we go from here.

Digging Myself a Little Hole

By Rachael Peckham

Three innings into my son's Little League game, I watch a freckled skinny kid called Fat Boy kick dirt with his legs the way a dog digs a hole. He's made considerable progress since the first inning, when the hole was only a soft depression at the foot of the bleachers, a place where a parent's feet might've gouged the ground every time her kid took the mound, stepped up to the plate. Fat Boy's mom sits directly behind me—I know because every couple of minutes she interrupts her cheering with a seamless order to stop kicking up dirt; you're shaking the bleachers; *now* what have you got?

He holds up a white nubby thing the size of a mechanical pencil eraser—in fact, I think it *is* a mechanical pencil eraser—and brags to his mom, "I found a tooth!"

"That's no surprise," she says, "in West Virginia."

It's one of those jokes I'm not sure I should laugh at, knowing full well it's not for me, the only one in these bleachers who mistakes the nearby town Hurricane for the natural disaster (*It's pronounced Hurr-a-ken, honey*); the only mother who doesn't sit on the top two rows (I sit at the end of the bottom bench), sharing a blanket that spans three laps, recounting a boss's hilarious flub at work, a cousin's called-off engagement, and always, their boys' windfalls and antics with teachers, with *WesTest*, with exes.

I keep my gaze focused on the mound, where my own son, Darius, takes a step and hurls a pitch at the plate. A hard throw, but it ricochets off the ground a foot or two in front of the batter, hitting him in the left calf. The boy jumps in place awhile before punching the plate once with his bat, releasing a puff of dust. I strain to hear if the error steals the conversation behind me and catch something—*This new rule about strikes*— but I can't make out the rest because Fat Boy has found a car-length piece of twine tied to the chain-link fence, and has taken hold of the loose end, encircling the smaller kids like a rancher does his cattle. And they love it. They squeal and buck their bodies against the lasso, and Fat Boy leans back on his heels, careful not to back into the freshly dug hole, at the same time, he realizes he can back his captors toward the freshly dug hole.

"Fat Boy, knock it off before somebody gets clothes-lined."

"I'm sorry," someone laughs. "How does a kid that skinny get the nickname Fat Boy?"

Thank God, somebody finally asked.

"He was a fat *baby*. Wasn't nothing he wouldn't eat." She pauses to yell something to her other boy—no nickname there—in right field. "When I call him by his real name, he just looks at me weird."

Fat Boy loosens his grip on the twine just enough for two older boys to seize the reins from him, turning it into a game of crack the whip. And I'm reminded of a memory I haven't thought about in years, when I was their age. When the brother of a friend horsed around with a dog leash in the yard. Then wore the leash as a joke. Then scampered up a tree, lost his footing, and the handle-end of the leash caught on a branch, breaking his fall. I was too young to go to Dustin's funeral, but I can still feel the edges of that fresh awareness like a punch to the thigh—that a *child* could die, at home, at play.

I will Fat Boy to drop the twine, to go back to pocketing teeth in his crater, for one of the mothers to pull a book out of her purse, even something electronic with beeps and chirps. I know I am wearing this thought when a mother scoots past me—"You boys are bothering people"—and breaks up the rodeo, pushing the pack toward the hill, Fat Boy trailing like a kite tail. They scurry to the top, then bowl their bodies down one after another, at the mercy of their own weight and their will, their need to fall. And nothing to get in the way of it except the sound of that ripe crack, when we all stop talking, and crane our necks, and somebody yells, "Heads up."

As If We Were Ancient Egyptians

By Andrea Bates

We buried my mother with the things she loved:
a teddy bear my father won at the county fair,
thick gold band the mortician had to glue
to her bony finger, urn of ashes from the dog

that had predeceased her. The attendant dressed
her in navy blue, the crepe pantsuit she had worn
at my sister's wedding. I was the scribe of her last
wishes, April afternoon when buds bloomed

and the kohl lining my eyes glistened:
twenty-third psalm, wreath of carnations,
Minister from St. John's Parish in Stamford.
No open casket. Some makeup.

The last one who saw her said how beautiful,
as if my mother were Lady Menhotep,
as if we had followed the embalming rituals
of the ancient Egyptians: removed the liver,

stomach, and intestines, had broken her brain
and hooked it through her nose. As if we had

let her bathe for forty days in natron, salt curing
the cancer from her body. As if we had swaddled

her skin to baby softness, scented the linen
with camphor and cinnamon, heart weighted
with a scarab amulet, inscribed with a spell
for going forth by day:

O my heart which I had from my mother,
O my heart which I had upon earth,
do not rise up against me as a witness
in the presence of the Lord of Things.

We would have inked her name on
the inside of the sarcophagus, arranged each
hand to cradle a roll of papyrus, poems
to bless her mouth in the afterlife.

Spider Webs

By Jamie Hoey

No one likes Uncle Reno. Mostly because he is forty and still lives with Grandma. Mostly because a forty-year-old man should not decorate his room with comic books and superhero action figures. Mostly because he is quiet and usually crabby. And mostly because he is an architect who complains about not having work, but never actually looks for any either.

Grandma is the only one who is okay with Uncle Reno's strangeness. Sometimes she still calls him "my little Reno" and babies him. Probably she still cuts up his food. He never leaves home for long. Except for one time he was gone for a really long time. Nobody ever told me where he went. No one likes to talk about Uncle Reno.

In the summers, sometimes Uncle Reno works at a concrete place making bricks. They make fancy shaped bricks, all different colors. I think Uncle Reno is strong to have to lift bricks all the time. But he said they use conveyor belts.

Uncle Reno is the reason Mom doesn't like to go to Grandma's house for Sunday dinners, but Daddy makes her go. It's tradition. One time Mom said we couldn't play with Uncle Reno because he isn't allowed by schools. I didn't know what she meant, but Daddy screamed at her to never say that again. I wish I wasn't allowed by schools. Uncle Reno doesn't want to play with us much though. Even on Sunday dinner days.

I like Grandma's house. Even though it smells like musty basement in the summer and I am not allowed to go into Uncle Reno's room per Mom. I look through the stacks of yellow hardcover National Geographic books about mountains, bugs, deer, Africa, the jungle, Antarctica, and fish. The bookcase is right by Uncle Reno's door and I try to peek inside his room every time he goes in and out. I like the shark book the best. Mostly because of the pretty pictures. Also, I like the monkey book. There is a picture inside of a line of monkeys that get taller and taller, and the last one looks like a man. One of the monkeys looks like my other uncle Dugan.

Nobody likes Uncle Reno because he never leaves home. But everyone loves Uncle Dugan even though he built a hermitage in Grandma's backyard. It looks like a little cabin, but he calls it his hermitage. Uncle Dugan has a long brown beard and wears plaid shirts and looks like a backwoodsman. His hermitage doesn't have electricity or running water, and he takes showers outside in the rain and drinks water out of barrels he puts under the eaves of his cabin. Everyone likes Uncle Dugan mostly because he is happy and jovial, and has two boys and two divorces.

Uncle Reno and Uncle Dugan are real brothers. My daddy is their brother, too, but not for real. Daddy said his dad got killed by a grizzly bear in Alaska when he was panning for gold. He tried to get away, but he slipped in the icy cold river and fell down, and the grizzly bear got him. Then Grandma married Uncle Reno and Uncle Dugan's dad, but his heart attacked him and he died, too. Maybe that's why Uncle Reno and Uncle Dugan don't leave Grandma. Parents are not safe by themselves.

One time Uncle Reno came over in the wintertime. I was playing outside with my red sled. Uncle Reno pulled me around and around in my sled very fast. Then we had a snowball fight, and I cried when I got hit. Mom came running outside yelling at Uncle Reno to stay away from me. She pulled me inside and asked if I was okay and did Uncle Reno try to touch me. She looked very scared and serious. I said no.

Mommy says to stay away from Uncle Reno because he isn't safe. She says this a lot.

Me and my sisters play games a lot. Mostly we play outside so Mom can have a break from us. She locks us outside. "Just for a half hour," she says, but then she watches her soap operas while we build teepees and run around the yard mostly naked. We have fun. Until the neighbors call Mom and she yells at us. She tells us to be "normal girls, who like to wear clothes and have tea parties." Whatever. We try that, but we drink so much red Kool-Aid that we get hyper from all the sugar and start laughing and burping, and then we pretend we are guys in a bar getting drunk. My sister Carrie gets apple juice for us and we pretend we're drinking beer.

Mom yells at us again.

My sister Carrie looks like my Uncle Reno who looks like Viggo Mortensen when he was in *Lord of the Rings*. Only Uncle Reno's hair is blonde and shaggy. Also he wears giant brown glasses. So mostly you have to really stare at him to make him look like Viggo. He doesn't like to be stared at. One time I told Carrie she was Uncle Reno's kid and she told Mom I said that. Mom screamed at me and told me never to say that again. She was very angry.

I change my story after that.

I tell Carrie that Uncle Reno had a wife once, and they had her. And then Uncle Reno's wife died, and he was so heartbroken that he gave Carrie to Mom and Daddy to keep. That makes Carrie cry. I tell her not to tell Mom. "This is a very sensitive issue to everyone. Everybody loved Uncle Reno's wife." I tell her this very seriously. "Don't say anything, Carrie, people might cry."

That is my secret story.

I used to be afraid of Uncle Reno a little bit. Because one time we were at Grandma's house, and I pulled the plug out of Carrie's Water Baby she named Moses (even though it was clearly a girl) and water came out of it, and Uncle Reno grabbed Moses and threw him into the bathroom sink. I thought he was mean. But when I made up the story about his wife dying, I felt bad for him. I tried to talk to him once, but he said he didn't like "little kid talk."

Mom throws a fit again when it is time for Sunday dinner. She throws a fit every Sunday. Daddy makes her go again. He always wins on Sundays, because the next day Mom gets a manicure. We go over to Grandma's house. She lives through the trees a little ways. Sometimes we walk, but mostly we drive. Mom says she doesn't like to carry the dessert through the woods. I don't think she likes to walk.

Grandma's kitchen has brown linoleum with white square bands and yellow flowers on it. Sometimes me and my cousin JJ, who is Uncle Dugan's boy, play slap-jack on the linoleum, but mostly he lives with his mom in Wawina. Uncle

Reno doesn't talk to anyone much. He stays in his room or sits outside smoking his pipe on the back step that is concrete. Maybe he misses bricks on Sundays.

Mom yells at us to go outside because we are being hyper. Grandma has dishes and dishes of Jolly Ranchers. We already ate a lot of them. My favorite flavor is Fire.

Grandma says, "Don't get all filled up on Jolly Farmers now!"

But why does she put them out every Sunday then?

We go outside and decide to have a beauty contest. I don't know why. First we ask Mom if she will be the judger, but she says, "I'm busy, go outside like I told you."

We ask Uncle Reno to be the judger. He says fine. Carrie can't walk straight and her arms fling too fast and she accidentally hits Uncle Reno's knee. She is out. I am relieved, just in case she is Uncle Reno's kid. At least he's playing fair. Lainey trips on a stick and falls over. I can walk in a straight line and so Uncle Reno picks me to be the beauty champion. He gives us all dandelions and we dance in circles. Except for Lainey, because she is mad she didn't win. Uncle Reno doesn't dance either. But he laughs and says we're crazy cats. Carrie starts meowing really loud, and we pretend we're cats for a little while. Uncle Reno watches us and lights his pipe. I like the smell of his pipe smoke. It smells like sweet vanilla, and the smell hangs all around him and falls off when he walks by you.

We get tired of playing cats and then play olly olly oxen free.

It's like hide-and-seek, but the hiders have to run to the picnic table and jump on it before the seeker can catch them. When you get to the table, you have to yell, "Olly olly oxen free!" as loud as your lungs can go. Uncle Reno says "fine," he will be the seeker.

We all run and scream, "Bloody murder!"

Mom yells out the window for us to stop yelling that and also for Uncle Reno to stop playing with us. I don't know why it's called screaming bloody murder if you can't actually scream those exact words. We scream it quieter after that.

When it is dinnertime, the adults sit at the big dining room table that has Grandma's fancy lace tablecloth on it and big burgundy candles wrapped in ivy and baby's breath in the center. Us kids sit on the brown linoleum and drink milk out of red, yellow, and lime green Tupperware cups with clearish sippy lids snapped on top even though we aren't babies. Grandma is very afraid of spills even though her carpet is brown shag and you can't even see the last spills I made in the corner by her plants.

There are pickles and pickled hot beans, carrots, olives, celery and dip, beets, boiled ham, mashed potatoes, potato salad, pasta salad, corn, and homemade rolls, brownies with fudge frosting, and cherry cake with vanilla drizzle. I fill up on butter and rolls and pickled hot beans. Uncle Dugan's mustache gets all white with potato salad. I think I see some egg in it, too—from breakfast maybe. Grandma tells him to use his napkin like a civilized person, but Uncle Dugan laughs and uses his sleeve instead. Grandma makes a frown at him.

"I'm going green," he says. But his shirt is blue, even I know that. After we finish the milk, Grandma rinses out our cups and gives us red Kool-Aid. Her Kool-Aid is the best because she mixes two packages of Kool-Aid and two coffee cups of sugar into one little pitcher. I tried making it at home that way once, but Mom got mad at me. Grandma gives us brownies and a piece of cake for dessert. I accidentally take off my sippy lid and try to drink like a big person. When I set my cup on the floor, Lainey knocks it over with her knee and the Kool-Aid rushes over Grandma's linoleum and all over our pants. I start to cry because now Mom will yell. Mom hears me crying and starts yelling.

"Why can't you kids behave? Why can't you eat and drink nice?"

Uncle Reno tells her to stop shouting. "It's just an accident," he says. "She didn't mean to spill."

Mom glares at Uncle Reno and tells him to raise his own kids. I look at Carrie. Her teal corduroy pants with the elastic band are red on the knees. My hands are stained red and sticky. Mom takes away my brownies and cake.

"No dessert for you; go outside."

I get up and go outside. I cry a lot. Mom doesn't understand. She just yells and bosses and watches soap operas. My chest hurts. I sit on Grandma's swing and dream about my heart attacking me. That would show Mom. She wouldn't yell at me again. Maybe she would play with us if I almost died. She used to help us paint pictures and make puppets, but she doesn't anymore, not after Lainey was born.

Uncle Reno comes around the side of the house. He puts his finger over his lips and wiggles his fingers for me to follow him. He smiles very sneaky at me. I get up and follow him behind Grandma's house. Sweet vanilla air falls off of him and swishes around in the breeze. Maybe we are playing hide and seek. Maybe we're going to be spies and sneak peeks at people through the windows. Maybe we will go on secret missions to steal Cheetos off of the counter when no one is looking. I am not scared.

Uncle Reno's shaggy hair fluffs when he takes a step.

Step, fluff, step, fluff, step, fluff.

We go all the way behind Grandma's house where Uncle Dugan's hermitage is peeking through the rosebushes and his outhouse is hidden by the hydrangeas.

On the concrete back step are two plates.

There are brownies and cake on the plates.

Uncle Reno sits down on the step and hands me a plate. "Don't tell your mom," he says.

I smile at him and tell him he has pretty eyes. They are sparkly and blue like Carrie's. He hunches his shoulders and grunts and eats his brownies. I eat all of mine. My chest doesn't hurt anymore. It feels happy. We eat our brownies first and then our cake. Uncle Reno eats the frosting with the cake, but I lick the vanilla drizzle off first, and then eat the cake. Mom's cake is good, but Grandma's brownies are way better than the ones we eat at school. I wish Grandma cooked at school.

"Uncle Reno," I say, "how come you can't go by schools?"

Uncle Reno's fork stops halfway to his mouth, then goes all the way back down to his plate.

"Because I gave a kid some candy and patted him on the head." Uncle Reno's voice sounds mad. But I laugh. He tells crazy stories.

"You're a crazy cat!" I say. Uncle Reno doesn't laugh, though. He just puts his plate down. A chipmunk runs out from under the rosebushes and looks at us.

"You try to be nice and you get in trouble," he says. He packs his pipe and lights it.

"Want a puff?" he looks at me and grins a little.

"No, thank you," I say. "Mom says that will kill you."

I think Uncle Reno says "good" really quiet, but then Mom yells, "Taylor, it's time to go!"

I give Uncle Reno my plate and try to give him a high five, but he doesn't give me one, so I hit him on the shoulder instead.

"Bye, Uncle Reno!"

He doesn't say bye.

When I wake up the next day there is a big spider web on our deck. The strings are all clear and silky shiny in the sun. Dewdrops sprinkle all of the threads, and sparkle with little rainbows inside of the drops. I stare at it for a long time. I think it's pretty. I run and get Mom to show her the rainbows and diamonds.

"Oh Taylor, that's gross!" Mom says, and knocks it down with a broom.

Aging August Rainfall

By Lakshmi Narayanan

It has been the warmest year for India in 108 years but now there is refreshingly cool news: The southwest monsoon is here . . .

—The Economic Times, *June 1, 2010*

more rain
rain strung like unbroken wicks
non-stopping
every day
and every night

permeating dampness
in the old house
built to stay dark and cool
through the sultry months
of april and may

unending rain
overstaying her welcome
wearing down aging parents
and grown children
who worry

that clothes
haven't dried in weeks
worry that tiles
in the leaking roof
will need replacing
worry that retaining walls
will wash away

worries unknown in
an earlier time
when rain was joy
an endless show to relish
from a windowsill

the rain-predicting bird peyum pakshi
continues its chorus
peyyum, peyyum . . .
it-will-rain, it-will-rain

The Pharmacy

By Marina Petrova

Your life, all stages of it, tragedies and triumphs, could fit onto a couple of pharmacy aisles. Good luck, girlfriend, the items on the shelves have been arranged for your convenience.

For the first few months, you will stay in the diapers, wipes, and baby bottles aisle. You are all set, as long as your diaper is dry and your stomach is not in a state of a violent uprising. Once you learn to crawl and realize that food is not always a liquid, you will move on to the aisle with little jars of yellow summer squash and boxes of Cheerios. Brace yourself. No matter how many times you spit out the summer squash, some unrelenting adult will be standing over you, ready to load the next spoonful into your mouth as if your name is Sisyphus. Hope it's not though; if it is, you already have a fairly large bone to pick with your parents.

You will spend the next few years in a rinse-wash-repeat cycle between the aisles with Halloween candy, sparkly holiday ornaments, and chocolate Easter eggs. With time, an invisible hand will crank up the dial with which the aisles turn. That's not your problem yet. Your problem is the adults who are no longer satisfied by your ability to smile and blow bubbles. They now expect you to make words out of letters and thoughts out of words. They will take you to the aisle with pens, pencils, and spiral notebooks. You will then go to school armed with a plastic lunchbox picturing a superfast talking racecar, Spiderman, or the Little Mermaid. You hope to meet them once you are old enough to drive.

Once you are old enough to drive, you will find out that superheroes do not exist and the Little Mermaid has been to rehab and is now working as the checkout clerk at the local Whole Foods. And you will move on to the next aisle—tampons and makeup. Anyone who says the trick to wearing makeup is to look like you are not wearing any has forgotten how it feels not to be taken seriously. Ignore them. Show up at the dinner table wearing heavy liquid eyeliner, dark purple eye shadow, and an orange lipstick. Your parents will have no choice but to treat you as an adult.

Don't bother with blush. Instead, sneak into the condom aisle and watch the color of your cheeks naturally turn from rosy pink to deep scarlet. If condoms have yet to see any action and blue is more your color, check out the beer aisle. Casually stroll down the aisle while dozens of beer bottles will cheer you on from behind the glass like parade spectators cheer on a Thanksgiving float. Pick a six-pack and find someone to buy it for you.

What's in the aisle between condoms and beer? Pregnancy tests. Tons of boxes neatly stacked on the shelf all promising an early response, assuming you want to know. Do you want to know? There are only two possible answers on this test. Regardless of the one you get, there is a 50 percent chance you will feel that you have failed. If the test is negative, breathe out and run. Or go back to the beer aisle. If it's positive, in a few months you will be right back where you've started—in the diaper aisle.

Diapers, baby bottles, wipes, bibs, more diapers . . . how many diapers can one nine-pound thing use in a week? Do the math quickly; before you know it, you will be standing in the next aisle buying birthday cake candles and pointy party hats. Picking party supplies the second time around, you know that you will need band-aids. What kind? Here they are again, the superheroes and the Disney characters. The Little Mermaid is winking at you from the top shelf, claiming she has not used for years. She lies. Just like you lie when you kiss a scrape or a bruise and promise it to make it better. Your kiss is nothing without band-aids and Neosporin. Forget the Little Mermaid and go with overachievers like Dora the Explorer or Thomas the Tank Engine. For years, Dora has been saving endangered penguins in the Antarctic, and Thomas has been getting high on the magical island of Sodor. You? You have been staring into your coffee cup for what feels like years, hoping to wake up in a different place when you get to the bottom of it.

Why are you always so tired? Perhaps the vitamin aisle can help. The shelf reads like a wall in a kindergarten classroom—A, B, C, D, E, F, G—Each letter promises to make your nails stronger, hair shinier, muscles leaner, legs faster, or sleep better. But you are already running as fast as you can and pass out cold when you hit the pillow. What you need is vitamin T for time. If you could only take it to make time stretchier and more elastic like a pair of control top pantyhose in the next aisle. As for your hair and nails, you will use the extra time for a deep conditioning treatment and a manicure.

While there are plenty of control top pantyhose in all colors and sizes, there is no vitamin T. If only you could stuff time into one super-strong, belly-holding pair. You cannot.

Time will spill out at the waistline into one gigantic muffin top, proving once again that control top pantyhose are nothing more than a marketing ploy.

In a few years, even vitamin T won't be enough, and you will find yourself walking, or limping, to the next aisle. That aisle is filled with over-the-counter remedies: antacids, painkillers, sleeping pills, and anti-inflammatory. Finally you got your kids under control, now your organs start to misbehave. You begin to compare notes with friends, meeting them in the waiting area by the prescription counter instead of that newly opened Asian fusion restaurant. Does their blood pressure fall and joints ache when it rains? You ask them how the surgery went, knee replacement or bypass, and how the recovery is going. You agree that recovery is tough and ask what the doctor prescribed.

In fact, the doctor has been churning out prescriptions like cheap summer beach reads, and you have been popping them like candy. You take them with food, before food, after food, or if you no longer like food, and then you buy yourself one of those plastic pill containers not to confuse the pills. You read about the side effects and double-check with the pharmacist in the window whether these medications can be taken together. The fonts on the pill jars keep getting smaller so you check out the stand with eyeglasses. Are you nearsighted or farsighted? Perhaps you are both and can only see objects placed exactly one foot in front of your nose, give or take an inch. There are glasses for that, too.

But no glasses can fix the fact that you no longer recognize your face when you look in the mirror. Who tied a couple of dumbbells to the corners of your eyes? How did your mother's smile, strained and uncomfortable, make its way to your face? You shake your head in disbelief and note that you have grown a turkey neck.

Still all is not lost, not until you find yourself standing in front of the adult diaper shelf. You've passed this shelf and snickered at it for years, so it would be ironic, to put it mildly, to find yourself in front of it now. Your mouth feels dry and you quickly scan the space around you to check if anyone is watching. And you thought buying condoms was embarrassing!

Do you still remember what you came here to buy in the first place? Your cart is packed with items you are no longer certain you need. You feel tired. After all, you've been to every aisle and now a hazy sleepy afternoon has wrapped itself around you making your eyelids very heavy . . . it is time to go. You head for the revolving door. But don't forget that there is a security guard at the exit sign and a cashier apathetically chewing gum behind the counter, waiting to scan all of your chosen goods.

The Guardians

By J. Watson Finger

The aroma of fresh baked cupcakes floated out the open kitchen window. Girlish laughter filled the small apartment.

"What kind of icing are you going to put on them?" thirteen-year-old Sana Fay asked, pointing toward the cooling round desserts on the tray.

"Half chocolate, half white icing, with squiggles all around." Cindy giggled. "Maybe I should put some peanut butter on them, too. And peanuts on the top."

"Oh no, don't." Sana Fay laughed. "Nobody will eat them."

"I will," the pudgy ten-year-old replied, reaching for another bowl to use for icing.

A loud rap on the front storm door interrupted the sisters' camaraderie. The girls looked out into the living room.

"Hello, Sana Fay. Is your mama here?" the white man asked, peering into the screen door. He was the third suitor who had knocked on their door and it was only ten a.m.

"Yes, sir, but she's not seeing anybody today," the older girl politely said.

"But I'm not just anybody. Tell her its Jack of Summerfield Goods and Notions," the man said curtly. His strong rough hand reached for the door handle.

"Yes, sir, but you can't come in and she's not feeling good today," Sana Fay said, never leaving her post by the front storm door. Her hand remained on the inside door latch. The man smiled, but his blue eyes coldly stared at Sana Fay for what seemed like an eternity. His face deepened into a dark red color as he released his hand from the door handle.

"Had a party last night, did she?" he asked angrily. "And what about you? Were you there as well?"

Sana Fay said nothing. Her facial expression revealed nothing, but she struggled to control her temper as she watched the rebuffed man leave the front yard and get into his car with the squealing wheels.

"Who was that?" a raspy voice shouted from a bedroom.

"Mr. Summerfield. He was really mad."

"Did he leave any money?"

"No, ma'am."

"Then he don't have a right to get mad. Damn him," the mother slurred. "Did y'all finish washing the clothes?"

"Yes, ma'am," the girls said.

"And folded all of the linens and put them away? Tomorrow I want the remaining clothes ironed. I'm going to work tomorrow, but it's only for a two-day job this week. I'm filling in for Florence Jean. She has a doctor's appointment and Miss Griffith won't let her take a half a day off. I don't want to look at the old lady myself, but Florence Jean needs her job. I'll help you with the ironing when I get home."

The next day, Sana Fay and Cindy woke at six a.m. to clean, cook, and iron clothes. It was summertime, but they still rose as if it were a school day. In the winter, the sisters performed their tasks before going to school. On weekends, it was the same before seeing their friends.

"Cindy, what are you cooking now?" Sana Fay asked.

"It's bacon and cheese egg pie," Cindy proudly announced. "I might enter it in the Girl Scout contest."

"Mama's not going to like you using up more breakfast food," Sana Fay warned. "Yesterday, you made smashed sweet potatoes with raisins, walnuts, peanut butter, and molasses. That stuff was awful! And last week it was hot dogs with cornflakes, onions, and crushed leftover barbeque chips and popcorn smeared in a mustard sauce."

"I didn't think it was that bad," the little girl said. "I forgot the hot sauce for the hot dogs."

"Oh, Cindy, you know molasses makes everything nasty."

"Aunt Flo said molasses was good for you."

"Aunt Flo eats fish bones and fish heads whenever she fries fresh fish," Sana Fay hollered.

Both girls began to giggle, then laughed loudly holding on to each other.

"Maybe I can put fish guts in something," mused Cindy in deep thought.

"You will get in trouble for this new project, Cindy. Remember the last time Mama discovered that you had tried a new recipe for pineapple, crabapple upside-down cake? You used all the sugar in the house. Mama was really mad when you gave all of the cake to the kids in the neighborhood."

"I borrowed the eggs from Aunt Flo and Miss Jenkins gave me the sausage. She's always knocking on the door asking for a cup of something."

"Yeah, Mama said her real name was Miss Cup of Sugar or Pinch of Salt Jenkins." Sana Fay laughed.

Later that evening, Cindy played jacks on the front stoop. Supper was long over, but the smell of sausage-onion-fried potatoes, and hot corn bread filled the apartment. The smell lingered outside.

Sana Fay quickly rode into the yard. Her hair was standing all over her head, sweat pouring from her face, a button missing from her blouse. She threw her bike violently on the ground.

"Mama home yet? Who cooked?" she asked, agitated.

"No, she's not. I cooked. What's wrong with you?"

"I got into a fight!"

"Again? You shouldn't be doing that. Just walk off like I do."

"Nobody's going to talk about my mama!"

"Hey, baby!" a loud voice shouted down the street. A stumbling figure meandered in the distance.

The girls ran from the porch. They gathered the woman in their arms, each holding or bracing the woman's body against their small shoulders.

"Come on, Mama, let's go in the house."

"I don't need any help. Just leave me alone. I can take care of myself. And you, too," she slurred.

"Yes, mama," they replied as they struggled to walk her onto the steps and into the house.

Playground, 1965: Yellow Hard as Brass

By Cynthia Clegg Canada

You stand by the playground fence,
laughing as you eat leaves
of poison ivy.
You are invincible,
indestructible—
immortal.
Your yellow hair glints as you toss your head,
your curls unbreakable.
Your fingers snap, snap, snap the stems,
stuff the leaves into your greedy, grinning mouth.
Your glee
is like Lucifer—
bright, shining, defiant, angelic
(and I mean that in the worst way).
Your socks don't match—you're starting a fad
so next week you can make fun of the rest of us.
I wish you were allergic after all.
Gleaming, gilded,
quicksilver liar,
pretender, manipulator—
fake—
The heart of you is hidden inside a hard shell
of yellow brass.

Lost and Found

By Susan E. Lindsey

Holly took a deep breath. The view from the ferry was astonishing—clear blue water, timber, and mountains dusted with late spring snow.

When Jake, her editor, told her he needed photos for a story on Stehekin, she was baffled. She had lived in Washington state all her twenty-eight years, but wasn't familiar with the tiny mountain community at the end of Lake Chelan. Jake said the magazine would pay for an overnight stay.

"I don't need to stay the night. Chelan isn't that far from Seattle. I'll just drive up, get the shots and come home."

"It's not that easy," Jake said. "You can't drive to Stehekin. You have to go to Chelan, then spend several hours on a ferry or catch a floatplane to the other end of the lake. It's a ferry, a plane, or a hike through the Cascade Mountains."

"You're kidding."

"Nope. That's the charm of the place. Gorgeous, quiet, remote—it's the kind of place people fantasize about when they want to get away."

A smile had crept over Holly's face. "When do I leave?"

Her timing was perfect; spring had come to the mountains. The lush deep green of Douglas firs contrasted with the brighter green of new leaves on the deciduous trees. From the ferry deck, Holly spotted a fawn grazing with its mother near the shore.

She dropped her backpack on one of the benches lining the ferry deck and pulled out her camera. She spotted an eagle and zoomed in; she captured his full wingspan and the silvery fish in his talons.

She picked up her gear and wandered the deck, shooting photos of the lake, forest, and other passengers. A couple leaned into one another by the railing. A little boy dragged his mother toward the stern to see the boat's wake. Two older men played cards and chatted. Everyone was in jeans, sweatshirts, and casual shoes. They looked more relaxed than Holly had felt in years.

Holly returned to the bench, sat down and dropped her pack beside it, but it wouldn't sit flat on the deck. She leaned over the arm of the bench and looked down. A purse lay between the bench and the bulkhead.

She awkwardly wrestled the purse over the armrest and a wallet fell into her lap. She picked it up and saw a name on an ID card: Anne Reeves. Holly inhaled sharply and memories flooded her mind.

Anne Reeves wasn't such an unusual name—there was certainly more than one person in the world with that name. But she immediately thought of her friend Anne. They were best friends all through school. "Thick as thieves," Holly's mom used to say. Anne spent half her childhood at Holly's place, even though Anne's dad was a doctor and they lived in a big, beautiful house.

Anne was tall and thin, with long red hair and porcelain skin that bruised easily. Holly still remembered the overnight stay in their sophomore year when she noticed the black and blue marks as they were both slipping on pajamas.

"Anne! What happened?"

Anne glanced at the purpling blotches on her arms, ribs, and thighs. She flushed.

"Nothing. You know what a klutz I am. I fell."

Holly remembered feeling vaguely distressed, but that was before people talked much about abuse. A few weeks later, after gym class, Anne whispered to Holly.

"I'm running away. Will you come with me?"

"What? What's going on?"

"I can't tell you; it's too private. But I have to leave. *Please* come with me."

The bell rang.

"Look, we've got to get to class. Come to my house after school. We can talk about it then."

Anne dropped her eyes. "Sure; that sounds good."

Holly never saw Anne again. Dr. and Mrs. Reeves reported her missing, and the police looked for a long time, but never found her. Months passed and then years. Anne's parents moved to another city.

The Anne-shaped hole in Holly's life lingered.

Now—running her finger over the familiar name in a stranger's wallet—Holly wondered again about Anne. What had happened to her? Would the story have had a different ending if Holly had gone with her or if she had told someone about the bruises?

Holly looked at the card; it had a Stehekin address. She decided to return the purse herself. She hadn't helped her Anne, but maybe now she could help another Anne in some small way. She tucked the wallet into the purse and the purse into her backpack.

The ferry landed, and Holly followed the other passengers off the boat. There were only a few cars in town and no taxis. Holly rented a bicycle and asked the bike guy for directions. She peddled north, past the bakery, the old schoolhouse, and Rainbow Falls. It had been forever since she had ridden a bike—the last time was with Anne.

"I guess it's true," she muttered to herself. "You never forget."

Holly spotted the yellow cottage right where the bike guy said it would be. Winded, she parked the bike, mounted three steps to the sagging porch, and knocked on the door. She glanced around. The setting was beautiful, serene, isolated.

She knocked again, wondering if she had the right house. But there weren't that many houses in Stehekin and this was the only yellow one she'd seen.

The doorknob turned. A tiny girl with copper curls stood there, clasping a stuffed dog.

Holly heard footsteps and a woman called out, "Sweetie, don't open the door to strangers."

A tall redhead stepped up behind the little girl. "Yes, may I help you?"

Holly stared into her eyes—Anne's eyes—and remembered the last time they had spoken: *I can't tell you. It's too private.*

"I found your purse on the ferry and I wanted to return it."

Holly handed the purse to Anne. Her fingertips brushed against those of her old friend.

Anne took the purse and thanked her.

Holly turned and descended the stairs. As she grasped the handlebars and prepared to swing her leg over the bike, she heard Anne say to her daughter, "Let's go in, Holly. It's a little chilly out here."

And Holly turned around.

Lessons in Seconds of Silence

By Mariam Williams

"Hey, can I ask you something?"

My friend laughs with fondness in response. Our nightly phone chats end with one of us posing some variation of that question so consistently now that he is no longer nervous about the half-second pause that precedes the preliminary inquiry.

"This is my favorite part of the night," he says. "Sure. Ask."

"Do you have any kids?" I rush the sounds out with just enough diction to distinguish each word from the next. I don't tell him my aunt had instructed me to ask him this to help me figure out his age, a number he had refused to give me when I had asked three weeks before.

"I have a son." One-second pause. "He's nineteen."

Longer pause. The longest pause ever registered in our dialogues since he called me two months ago, saying he felt like we started a conversation nearly a year ago that we never finished.

"And there's silence," he says, dismay bleeding through the phone.

I flounder for words, a problem my detailed cell phone bill would indicate has never before existed with him. "Wow. That's . . . surprising. That's really surprising," I gasp.

My eyes widen and I run my hand over my face and pace the floor as I start doing the math in my head. The man I saw perform live in a show requiring him to sprint, sing, and stomp for nearly two hours without ever leaving the stage had a what? The saying goes, "Black don't crack," but his personal training side hustle, mixed martial arts hobby, occasional vegan habit, and bohemian artist-like happiness must have enhanced the melanin's powers. I knew he wasn't twenty, or even my age then of twenty-nine, but a nineteen-year-old son? Am I wrong for hoping he was having unprotected sex at around age fifteen?

I hear him telling me he and his son's mom divorced when the child was two. Hope evaporates. I recalculate.

His son's existence and age were things he wanted to tell me in person, he says. Then he asks, "How do you feel about all this?"

"I don't know," I reply. I catch a glimpse of myself in the mirror. I look like Wile E. Coyote after yet another Acme Corporation anvil has landed on his head as the Road Runner he was trying to crush with it laughs. "Beep, beep."

"It's not the first time I've—I'm sorry. I don't know the appropriate verb here."

I know the word for what we're doing exists in the English lexicon, but I don't know what it is. We're not dating; he's in New York, I'm in Kentucky. A year has gone by since we last saw each other, and until recently, we've thought of each other in only a professional context. We are pursuing a relationship, maybe, but that reveals too much of my expectations. Flirting definitely, but what if that minimizes what it could be? Getting to know each other so we can figure out if we want to act on our flirtations and start a relationship that's more than a friendship. Perhaps there is no word for whatever this is.

My brain processes those thoughts in a nanosecond, any noticeable silence absent, and I continue, "Talked to, I guess, since talking is what we're doing right now. So it's not the first time I've talked to a man with an adult . . . child."

In the seconds of silence that follow our awkward good-bye, I throw my head back and laugh as I think of an ex-boyfriend eighteen years my senior, divorced, and with a son exactly my age. I wonder why I've chosen the same man again and what lesson I evidently still need to learn.

Maybe the lesson is to let my imagination run away when I write plays, but to face reality with people. I had pictured shameless public displays of affection that would have everyone buzzing at the theater festival for which my latest suitor was returning to Kentucky. In another two years, a play we co-wrote would debut there. We would become a theater power couple whose story couldn't be more fitting: romance blossoms between two writers, one also an actor, the other watching from the audience. Imagine how creative their kids will be!

In reality, my verbiage was correct. He and I were talking, and that was it. Yes, he had admitted he was attracted to me that night in the bar ten months ago when we discussed our work for two hours. Yes, his choice not to speak to me at all, even as a friend, until after the relationship he was in then had ended told me his attraction was strong enough for me to have been a threat. He did say my city was among those he was considering moving to within the next six months, and that he was looking for a place to settle down. When I mentioned needing to save money for a friend's wedding in Houston, he asked the wedding date, because he would be performing there in September—seven months in the future. So what if we had talked so much that he ran through his allotted monthly cell phone minutes and about six months of accumulated rollover minutes, and lost his voice on stage? His adult son cannot affect a non-existent romance, and I should guard my heart.

My yoga instructor presents a different lesson the next morning. She says we often dread exercise because we use it to beat ourselves up instead of creating experiences we want to repeat.

I begin to think my lesson is to not allow factors like age or whether a man has children to interfere when my heart feels alive. In the last several months of my relationship with a man who fit a multitude of perfect-man criteria, I grimaced when I saw his name appear on my Blackberry's screen. We argued daily, he eventually told me I was no longer fun to talk to, and my heart stopped pumping for him.

As I move through my yoga practice, I realize I don't dread getting a phone call from this man who's been an adult a little longer than the last one. I smile when I see his texts alerting me that he's arrived safely at every stop on his show's tour. He has already said, "The more I talk to you, the more I want to talk to you," and I feel the same way. I am on the edge of happiness, and I'm prepared to let it go because there's an unexpected complication in my vision of perfection? If fantasizing about the future was stupid, this is even worse—and yet I do it all the time. I routinely abandon plans that haven't gone "right," as if I could demand flawlessness from the weather, traffic, other people, or from myself, and I find comfort in the familiarity of disappointment. The pleasure I have felt after a few weeks of conversation is *good*, and I don't want it to stop.

Perhaps, then, it is time for me to learn to create experiences I want to repeat.

I break the silence that has now spanned two days. I call and tell him that the existence of his nineteen-year-old son doesn't change how I feel.

"How did you decide that?" he asks.

"In yoga," I say. "But I'll tell you more about it when you get here."

Arctic Reflections

By Emily Boone

Arctic Kayaking

Like an orange turned inside out, the Arctic waters seem to expand.
An ephemeral rainbow draws my eyes to black island remnants.
Glacier tracks dwarf my sense of time.
The never-setting sun erases my compass.
The encapsulating sparseness magnifies my solitude.
Inhale. Exhale. Listen. Experience Svalbard's journey.
Traversing the planet from the Antarctic to the Arctic;
　　　Svalbard's compass is present.
My compass re-emerges.

Hidden Life: Spitzbergen, Svalbard

Travelers so accustomed to multitudes
　　　do not see minutiae.
Willow trees smaller than a thimble
Sorrell full of vitamin C
　　　postpones a scurvy death
All unnoticed, trampled underfoot.

Stillness Sometimes: The Hinlopen Strait

Melting ice, sun edging over the horizon, swift cold currents
Illuminate the frozen land and sea.
The Arctic stirs under the never-setting sun
Whales and birds arrive and gulp the bounty.
The cycle of birthing, preying, ingesting, expiring
        is continuous until the sun disappears over the horizon,
        then waves freeze and the stillness returns.
Death brings life in the Arctic.

Expedition Good-byes

This Arctic silence creeps into each traveler
        spreading an undetected cellular camaraderie.
Now, parting approaches and we are stunned by our bonds.
This silence crept in and encompassed the expedition
Just as fog surrounds and leads to inner fjords . . .
        penetrating deeper than ever envisioned.
Our journey has just begun as we wave good-bye.

Reluctant Citizens

By Peggy Grimes

We tend to forget that all refugees come with a history of their own, and some don't really want to be here. They may be forced to our shores by someone else's motives. And we cannot really know their level of fear, nor their inner ability to cope. My church took on the risk of helping some of these people who were forced to leave home for a new life in America.

I walked into the meeting room as inconspicuously as I could. I knew they needed me, and was not sure I had the time to commit to this project. But I was curious. One of the sweetest ladies of the church asked me to come and I could not turn her down. When Anne saw me slip into a chair on the back row, she signaled me to sit beside her near the front.

Our young assistant priest, David, was reviewing the names and histories of the three refugees we were getting from Fort Chaffee, Arkansas. A fourth one was possible, but we would learn about him later. Many of us had thought these would be families with children we could get involved in the church, the schools, and the community. But it soon became clear that these refugees were all men. Some parishioners left the meeting disappointed.

All were Cuban refugees to whom our church had decided to offer a home, comfort, and support in a strange land. The shocking fact was that most did not want to come at all. But in 1980, Fidel Castro had decided to send certain of his citizens to the US in a gesture of "goodwill." He had ordered some 20,000 men to the beach at Mariel and shipped them all to Miami, Florida. They became known as the Marielitos. Clearly defined as refugees, the United States government had accepted them, but knew they would flood Miami with a population bubble the city could not support. Therefore, if they did not have relatives who could take them in, they were sent to Fort Chaffee, Arkansas. From there, they would be dispersed to various parts of the country where they could find jobs and be gradually integrated into the population. Many churches decided to take a responsible role in this effort, offering housing and training for them to become productive citizens. Our church, St. Matthew's Episcopal Church, was one of them. A committee of members stepped forth to see this through. None of them spoke Spanish. That is why they needed me.

David described the first man, Eduardo. He was in his late forties, spoke some English, and had a family in Cuba that he was leaving behind. He had a wife and two sons, one thirteen and one sixteen. He was told he must leave them behind forever. All the family would thereby be taken care of, and the sons would automatically go into the army at the correct age and have a career. His sacrifice would ensure their safety. He had been a cook for many years, but had not spoken well about Cuba and complained openly about the lack of means to do better for oneself. They were tired of it, and forced him to the beach of Mariel. We believed that this man had a good chance to make it, blessed with beginning language skills and a good job. He might be independent sooner than most, and become a productive, happy citizen.

The second man was Alejandro. He had no family. He spoke no English. He had been a Jehovah's Witness and had suffered many stints in prison because he would not swear allegiance to the communist party. He later explained that if you did not work in Cuba for two weeks, the government forced you into a job. If you did not work well, or chose to abandon the rules, you went to prison. He had been in several prisons. His skill level was unknown.

I looked around the room at the people who had pledged support. They were asking perceptive questions, and were assessing the practical issues. These were people of the East End, "Indian Hills" variety; men of prominence in the business community and polished ladies of grace and education who were quiet about their service. While I knew our church was active in community outreach, I could scarcely believe who was actually there to answer this call. A lot of hands-on work would be required and it could get ugly. As details unfolded, they were willing to take this chance. I was impressed.

The third man on the list was Francisco. He was described as a man of the streets. He drank too much, caroused too much, was a drain on society's goodwill, and had no ambition. He had a sister with multiple sclerosis who lived with him. He was responsible for all her care. He was taken to the beach and told that his sister would be well cared for by the government on the condition that he leave the country forever.

He boarded the boat with all the rest. He, too, spoke no English.

The fourth man, Alberto, was nineteen years old. We were told little about him except that he wanted to live life out of the city and was in need of a new start. He spoke no English. We might get him or might not. We offered some support for him if he were shipped to our area. As it turned out, a farm family in Indiana spoke up for him. He could live with them and help with the animals and chores. It seemed like the perfect match. Someone would keep tabs on his progress.

These men all arrived within the week. The committee had been very diligent in getting an apartment for each, furnishing it with secondhand furniture from the congregation, getting essential appliances and food into the refrigerators, and lining up jobs. Eduardo and Alejandro shared an apartment. Francisco lived alone. Each had a contact person who took responsibility for checking on them every day and getting them to English class or to work. It was an impressive commitment.

Since I was still working, my job was limited to being an emergency helper if a real problem arrived and they needed a direct translator. Each group would have to strive to communicate as individuals, whether Spanish to English or English to Spanish. It was considered a mutual struggle that would bring them closer together. Everyone made use of the help and the Cubans began to feel better about gradually speaking a little English. In the beginning, they learned to answer simple questions, take directions at work, and were responsibly on time, which is not usually a reliable Latin trait.

Then we began to hear that Eduardo was feeling despondent. He missed his family and wanted to speak to them. He was drinking too much at night. Someone managed to arrange a phone call to Cuba. It helped him. Then letters began to arrive for him. It made him feel he could keep in touch. His job as a cook was going well. It looked like he might be building a career. Our hopes rose.

Alejandro did well also. He was acquiring English faster than anyone expected. He was working with a painting contractor who praised his work and quizzed him on vocabulary of the workplace all day. Each was beginning to make his own money, buy his own clothes, go to the grocery alone, and find evening entertainment. We didn't worry much about exactly what that was until David got a call from Alejandro. It seemed Eduardo was stoned on drugs. David went over to see them and explained the kind of trouble he could be in by getting into drugs. This could ruin their chance at a new life and their freedom. It could even reverse the good agreement under which they were granted asylum, or land him directly in prison. It seemed the message was received well.

A few weeks later, Eduardo was in jail on a drug charge. He was bailed out by the committee and ordered to counseling with a Cuban-born psychiatrist who volunteered to help. This wonderful doctor really tried to get Eduardo on his feet, but the despair over losing his family could not be overcome. Eventually, he was caught dealing drugs and arrested. He was then sent to prison on multiple charges. We had thought that Eduardo had the most potential for making a successful transition and becoming a good citizen. We were wrong.

On the other hand, Alejandro became determined to make his new life one of success. He quit working for the contractor and started his own painting enterprise. First, he asked people from the church for jobs in their homes, and then got referrals to other homes. Harry and I hired him to paint our whole downstairs. He did a wonderful job. While he painted, he talked to me about his life in Cuba. I will never forget the mental pictures.

He had worked in swamps catching alligators, on farms harvesting crops; he had cut sugar cane and had all kinds of government-assigned jobs. He said he was only allowed to own two shirts, two pairs of pants, and two pairs of shoes. If he made enough money to get something really nice to wear, to go out in the evening with friends, he had to give up one of the other pieces of clothing. He also said that because he would not swear allegiance to the communist party, they imprisoned him in a box like they use in the morgue . . . a drawer. He was kept there six months, rolled out once a day for half an hour to go to the bathroom and eat a meal, then rolled back into the dark. He maintained his sanity by reciting to himself poems he knew and Bible stories. He did not share the details of other brutal treatment. Though charming and personable, he had a stubborn core. We were sure he would survive.

Alejandro met a Guatemalan woman who was a maid for one of our parishioners. They fell in love and got married. After living in Louisville a year, they moved to Texas where she had relatives. They now have a son. I am sure they are both successful citizens.

Alberto, the nineteen-year-old, was not checked on frequently. In the beginning, it appeared that he was doing well. The contact would see him in the fields plowing on a tractor or feeding livestock. The farm family gave rave reviews, but no one spoke directly with Alberto for a while. Then the Cuban doctor went out to see him and found him ready to commit suicide. He had not learned any English. The family hardly spoke to him. He had been living in the barn without human contact except to be put to work, and even ate his meals alone. The doctor removed him immediately from the family, sent him to the hospital for psychiatric help, and then returned him to Fort Chaffee.

This thoughtful experiment was feeling like good intentions gone bad. Two of the four men had landed in bigger trouble than when they arrived.

The fourth man, Francisco, was a surprise altogether. We couldn't help feeling great dread about this man of the streets, who brought an ominous reputation with him. He was going to be trouble. He had a way of getting a job, losing it, yet always having money to find a bar and drink too much.

One night at eleven o'clock, my phone rang, and it was David. "Peggy, do you think you could help us out tonight? Francisco is in trouble and I need a translator."

"Sure, David, where are you?"

"Do you know where the Dew Drop Inn is? It is down on Story Avenue near the stockyards."

"Yes, I do because I pass it on my way to work each morning. What has happened?"

"Well, Francisco is drunker than a skunk and has started a fight. The police were called and no one understands what he is saying. He needs an advocate and a translator. Can you come down?"

I drove down Brownsboro Road and on towards the stockyards. I could see the two patrol cars with flashing lights outside the Dew Drop Inn and parked as close as I could. Walking toward the bar, I spotted David and a couple of people standing with the police; then I saw Francisco in handcuffs next to the patrol car. When he saw me, he called out to me in a slurred garble, and I responded with a careful greeting.

David stepped up and thanked me for coming, saying he needed to explain to Francisco what he was charged with and then get his side of the story. The policeman said he was drunk and disorderly, and had caused a bar fight. They had been called to the scene because of Francisco. He was under arrest. I told all of this to him in Spanish, not sure if he could comprehend it in his weaving stupor. He cursed back, saying he had been treated awfully bad, and was harming no one. I asked what his side of the story was. He said he liked women with big breasts and had reached out to touch one. The woman had not responded nicely, he said. She punched him, and then others joined in. When the police arrived, they dragged him to the sidewalk.

The policeman then told me he had been difficult to subdue. Once they thought he had cooled down, he turned to the patrol car and urinated on it. They handcuffed him and added a charge. I explained it all to Francisco who denied nothing. David asked for the details of what would happen next. They put Francisco into the car and took him off to jail.

The next morning, David and I went to the hearing and were able to bail him out. On the way home, I explained how serious this pattern of behavior was in the eyes of our law, and that we could not keep doing this. He must change his habits.

Of course, we knew these habits had been his all along. There was little hope.

The committee met and decided that Francisco was a hazard. If we did not want him jailed forever, he would have to go back to Fort Chaffee to be rehabilitated by some other means. We would pack him up and send him out on a flight today. He would be met by authorities at the other end.

Four of us arrived at his apartment to explain it all to him and move the plan forward. We would pack him up and take him to the airport. Francisco met us with a serious expression on his face, but sober. I translated for David.

"The committee has determined that your behavior has caused us to withdraw our support for you in Kentucky. We have arranged for you to be returned to Fort Chaffee this afternoon. You will be given another place to go from there."

Francisco replied that he would not return to Fort Chaffee and we could not make him go. Well, this was right. We couldn't.

"Then you will be completely on your own, no matter what happens with the law. Your rent is paid until the end of the month, but after that, you will be responsible."

He agreed and we left.

We heard nothing about him for weeks and wondered what happened to him. Then one Sunday, he arrived at church with a girlfriend. Yes, she fit his physical requirements, although missing some teeth. Something new was going on. He said he wanted to come to church to let us know he was changing. He stopped drinking, had a job, and was grateful for all we had done. To thank us, he wanted to do some cleanup yard work around the grounds, weed and rake, do anything we needed. Of course, we were glad to have him and he did deliver on his promises.

He later married his girlfriend at our church. David officiated. She wore a white, street-length dress. He wore an all-white formal suit of tails. No one knows where he got that outfit. A couple from the committee stood as their witnesses and members of the congregation attended. It was sweet and simple. They went on to live their new life together and later had a baby. The true surprise was that this most hopeless of all four refugees found a new life, hope, and happiness in a country intended to be his punishment

We like to think that life in America is good, and that all the world wants to be here. But it is not always so. We can give help and guidance, rescue, and a home. But success depends on the individual who comes with his own complications. It is sad that only two of these four men made the transition. The others were destroyed by it.

Axed

By Susan E. Lindsey

Carla grabbed the leash and clipped it onto Beast's collar.

"Come on, boy," she said. "We're going for a walk. It's cold out, but it will do us good."

She opened the cabin door and let the enormous Newfoundland out. The late afternoon sky was steel gray and icy wind blew across Loon Lake. It was supposed to freeze solid tonight. She was staying in a vacation cabin in northern Minnesota; rent was pretty cheap in the winter.

Carla walked to the little resort store—the only place around to buy groceries. She tied Beast to the bike rack and headed into the overheated store.

"Hi, Jimmy," she said to the clerk.

"Hey, Carla! Any news on a job?"

"Yeah, but none that's good."

"Sorry. I know it's tough out there right now."

Carla carried two cans of cheap soup, an apple, a loaf of generic bread, and a quart of milk to the counter. She pulled ten dollars out of her pocket.

"Want a lottery ticket?" Jimmy asked. "It's up to $12 million."

"Sure, but let me pick my numbers." Carla rarely played the lottery and always chose the same numbers.

"Good luck!" Jimmy said.

Carla smiled wanly at him and pushed the ticket into her pocket. She grabbed her groceries, stepped outside, and untied Beast.

"Good luck?" Carla muttered. "I haven't had *good* luck in years!"

She thought about it—the layoffs at work, the wreck that totaled her car, the unemployment lines, the failed cupcake business, and dozens of job applications. She had no job, no prospects, no car, and no health insurance. She had some cash, but it wouldn't last more than a few weeks.

"Beast, you better start developing a taste for squirrels," she said.

She and Beast walked to the end of the boat dock. She sighed, took a deep breath, and closed her eyes, trying to let her worries slip away.

Beast barked at a lone Canadian goose on the lake and yanked on the leash around her wrist. Suddenly Carla, the dog, and the groceries were in the freezing water. She released the leash, and Beast swam a few feet away, barking at the goose as it flew into the sky.

Carla kicked off her heavy shoes and swam to the dock. Beast lumbered up onto shore and shook water out of his thick, black coat.

Carla shivered uncontrollably. She jogged to the house with Beast trailing her. Inside, she toweled off the dog, then stripped off her wet clothes and jumped into a hot shower. Fifteen minutes later, she stepped out, dried herself, and pulled on a heavy sweater, sweatpants, and thick socks. She dried her hair, teeth still chattering.

She stepped into the kitchen, pulled open a cupboard door, and grabbed a bottle of Christmas sherry. She didn't especially like sherry, but desperate times call for desperate measures. She poured some into a mug and carried it and the bottle to the ratty couch. She knew better than to drink on an empty stomach, but her dinner was in the lake.

Carla curled up under an afghan. She sipped the sherry and was startled to find tears rolling down her face. She sniffled, sobbed, drank a little more, and then a lot more.

Carla groaned and opened one eye. Morning sun filtered through the cheap blinds. She rolled off the couch and headed to the bathroom, and then into the kitchen to make coffee. While Mr. Coffee sputtered, Carla opened the front door and let Beast out. She picked up the newspaper and unfolded it: "Loon Lake store sells $12 mil ticket." Her eyes flew open and she scanned the paper until she found the winning numbers.

She ran to the pile of clothes on the bathroom floor and dug through all the pockets. She came up with only a soggy tissue. She threw on a jacket and shoved her stocking feet into her slippers, bemoaning the loss of her shoes. She ran outside.

The lake was a sheet of blue ice, gleaming in the morning sun.

She ran toward the dock, sliding on the icy ground. Beast raced in circles around her, barking madly. At the shore, she tested the ice. It seemed solid. She stepped onto it and slid along to the end of the dock.

She glanced down, alert for cracks. Suddenly, she tensed and dropped to her knees. There it was—the bright yellow lottery ticket suspended just under the surface. Desperately clawing at the ice, she screamed, "No, it's not fair!"

Carla jumped to her feet and ran to the cabin. She grabbed the ax she used for firewood and raced back to the lake. She dropped to her knees again and banged away. It was no good; the ice was too thick. She stood up—and channeling two years of frustration—swung the ax as hard as she could.

Carla's bandaged foot was propped up on a stool.

Jimmy handed her a glass of sherry.

"You know, it's OK," she said. "I have nine other toes. And $12 million covers a lot of health care."

Military Experiences

By Emily Boone

Loyalty to Whom

Do I know myself?
The army recruits resources to implement its mission.
Soldiers are an indispensible and dying resource.
I am a soldier. Now is past the time to question.
I did not know the questions before I enlisted.
Now is too late to ask or make other choices.
The answers for all legitimate concerns are:
　　　Duty first. Be loyal. Sharpen resiliency skills.
These sufficiently address acknowledged concerns.
When my enlistment is finished, I can have a life.
For now—be numb; don't question; follow orders.
Hopefully, I will survive my impulsive, possibly lethal choice.

The Complete Community or Residential Treatment

The fort's motto, "Strength begins here," is my core.
Brigade's motto, "Duty first," is my daily to-do list.
My only decision is how quickly to implement orders.
The army supplies everything for me and my family:
　　　Meals, daily schedule, sanitation, housing, schooling,

recreation, physical health care, evangelical religious care,
window-dressing managed mental health access,
trauma cures using resiliency skills.
Life is very simple. Just follow orders. No learning curve here.
Do I really know me? Is knowing me even desired here?
Am I to be considered? Do I even exist?

A Day at the Mall

By J. Watson Finger

The three girls' laughter filled the mall breezeway. They spoke at once, pointing at the new spring fashions in the store windows. They looked odd, a rainbow of colors. One girl was tall, thin, and blond. Another girl was a petite build with red hair, and the other a pudgy, dark-skinned girl with short, nappy hair. They were cousins, cousins who lived as sisters, cousins who shared clothes and middle school supplies. And today, the first day of spring break, they were free to do as they pleased.

"What if Dad finds out?"

"Whose dad? My dad is in prison." Tia shrugged.

"Then that eliminates him. You don't have anything to worry about, Tia," Ashley said sharply as she tossed her long blond hair.

"No, I'm talking about my real dad. He won't like this at all. He's proud of me," the red-haired girl whined.

"Sure, sure," Jasmine whispered under her breath. "Your dad cares so much about you."

The threesome walked into the department store, eyeing the makeup counter.

"Remember our plan," Ashley drilled. "Tia is to go to the accessory department and Jasmine will go to the cosmetic section. I'm going to the teen area. Then we will have what we want. It's easy."

The girls followed their instructions like lambs led to slaughter.

But Jasmine's mind was on other things. "I need deodorant and sweet-smelling soaps and products to manage my coarse hair. Mom said braids cost too much," she mused, as she touched her wiry hair, thinking of Alicia Keys, the R&B singer. Jasmine picked up bottles of perfume, spraying on the inside of her arm as she had seen her mother do prior to countless dates throughout the week. On the weekends, Jasmine's mother stayed with her boyfriend, and Jasmine was usually alone or with her grandmother.

"May I help you?" the lady said, in a cold, crisp voice. She looked at the young girl with disdain.

"No, ma'am. I'm just looking," Jasmine sheepishly said. The saleslady frowned, but did not move. Jasmine quietly moved toward the makeup selections. There were numerous samples of colors on display. She dabbed her finger in three of them as she looked into the display mirror.

"I can look as beautiful as my cousins," she said as looked at the reflection of dark brown skin in the mirror. She glided the glossy substance onto her lips, much too red, but she did it anyway. She glanced both ways as she slid the makeup into her purse. She saw more perfume and placed it into her cache, too.

"They don't have black products here, but I can use my cousins'," she said proudly, although she knew their makeup was for white skin.

Tia and Ashley were waiting outside of the storefront entrance as Jasmine exited the store. Just as she smiled, the male voice said, "Young lady, please come with me and open your purse."

Jasmine froze. Her cousins watched, but moved away from the store entrance.

"Call your parents if you have a cell phone," the security guard said.

"My cousin has my phone," she said, as she watched her cousins walk away from the store.

"Then I will call for you."

The young guard dialed her mother's number, but there was no answer. He tried her father's number, but with the same results.

Jasmine spent the night alone at the detention center. She was an A student, never been in trouble. She cried and waited and cried some more. The next morning, a loud forceful voice echoed down the hall. Nana!

"Don't tell me why you're here. I know those young rattlesnakes are behind it! Jazzy, people lay in the sun for hours craving what you have, beautiful dark skin. You are my special grandchild, the best of the bunch," Nana said, as she wrapped her white arms around Jasmine's shoulders. Jasmine sighed.

Your Call Is Very Important: A Telephone Play

By Emily Boone

CHARACTERS

AUTOMATED ANSWERING SYSTEM

CALL CENTER OPERATOR

CLIENT

AUTOMATED ANSWERING SYSTEM

Welcome to ARECC: Accessible Reliable Excellent Competent Counseling . . . the go-to service center for your mental health needs. You are in good hands with ARECC, and your confidentiality is guarded with dedication. Your call is very important to ARECC.

So that ARECC may serve you better, please listen carefully to all the options before you make a selection as our options have recently changed; or you can go online to www.ARECC.org and very quickly get the information. If this is an emergency, hang up and dial 911 immediately.

Otherwise, please listen to the following options.
If you know your party's extension, press one.
If you are a subscriber, press two.
If you are a provider, press three.
If you are a facility seeking pre-authorization, press four.
If you are seeking to become an in-network provider with ARECC, press five.
If you are calling about claims, press six.
If you are updating your contact information, press seven.
All other callers please hold for the next available assistant who will be with you shortly.

(Silence for three seconds)

AUTOMATED ANSWERING SYSTEM

Are you still there? I did not hear a response. Your call is very important. ARECC can serve you better if you will do one of the following. Please press eight to repeat the menu. Press star to exit.

(Silence for three seconds)

AUTOMATED ANSWERING SYSTEM

Are you still there? I did not hear a response. Your call is very important to ARECC. ARECC wants to be responsive to your phone call. I will get an associate on the line. I can get you to the correct ARECC associate, if you will enter your subscriber ID number using the telephone key pad.

(Phone sounds as nine numbers are entered)

AUTOMATED ANSWERING SYSTEM

Now, using the key pad, enter the subscriber's birth date, using the format of two numbers for the month, the day, and the year. This gives ARECC the information to get you to the most appropriate associate.

(Phone sounds as the six numbers are entered)

CALL CENTER OPERATOR

Hello, my name is Rhonda, your ARECC associate, and my ID number is 5349. Did you know that you can get information online at www.ARECC.org?

CLIENT

My name is Matthew Hayes and I prefer to talk to a human about counseling. I am calling to get authorization to talk to a counselor because I feel so depressed. Can you help me?

CALL CENTER OPERATOR

I can help you, but first I must have your ARECC member ID number and several pieces of information.

CLIENT

I just punched in my ID number before you came on the line. Did that information get forwarded to you?

CALL CENTER OPERATOR

I'm sorry, sir. No information was forwarded to me. Your call is very important to ARECC. ARECC is here to give you fast service. Now, just answer these several questions beginning with your ID number and date of birth.

CLIENT

How many times do I have to give the same information before I am issued an authorization number?

CALL CENTER OPERATOR

ARECC will provide you with the relevant information after you provide your ID number, birth date, address, place of employment, insurance plan name, group number, number of years with the company, and the last four of your social. Shall we get started? Or you can access this information online at www.ARECC.org.

CLIENT

I need to talk to a counselor. Why is getting an ARECC referral is so difficult?

CALL CENTER OPERATOR

Mr. Hayes, ARECC is here to help you if you will only answer these fifteen questions. It is just a matter of getting started. What is your birth date?

CLIENT

I am becoming a wreck going through all these questions. I just want the authorization to talk to a counselor under my ARECC insurance.

CALL CENTER OPERATOR

Mr. Hayes, ARECC requires you answer these fifteen questions. That's all. Shall we begin?

(Dial tone sounds)

CALL CENTER OPERATOR

Hello? Hello? Is anyone there? ARECC is here to serve you with accessible, reliable, expert counseling. Hello? . . . Hello?

(Dial tone continues)

Our Brother

By Carroll Grossman

A son, a father, a friend, and brother
Passed from life to death
earth to heaven
flesh to spirit
His melody on earth complete.

He leaves sons who grieve
Who lament his death and his debts,
question how to plan his good-bye.
Hugs, tears, laughter, comfort.
Hold the cost. Pass the plate.

In the protocol of funerals
immediate family seated in front
brothers of the deceased nearby.
Aunts, uncles, nieces, nephews, cousins
fall in place in the next pews.
Friends and business associates
find their places.

Who is standing near the open casket?
Ex-wife number one, hugging a son.
Followed by another former wife,

tugging, wringing a lace hanky.
Ex-wife three—tentative, at the door.
I watch, wait
Where do they sit?

Scene II

The former wives find seats
One steps gingerly over legs and feet
finds a place in back, near the wall,
another sits left of center,
the third near a friendly cousin

The eulogy begins.
Family, friends, brothers, and sisters
We gather here today to celebrate
the life of our dear departed brother.
The minister pauses to read the obit.
Now, Harry. He meant a lot to me.
And, here's the deal. Harry was a good man
Oh, he did some things he shouldn't have;
I've done things I shouldn't have.
But Harry reached out, touched people.
A wife nods, all three nod.
He sang in the choir, he helped at church,
always the last to leave.
A good man, a good friend.

We had lunch. We talked about stuff.
All the important stuff.
Stuff we didn't share with others
I won't say more.
The preacher wipes his eyes
Reads Bible verses. Delivers a message.
It is only Harry's physical self that's gone.
It's our loss, not Harry's.
He's in a better place.
Shaking hands at the pearly gates
Now here's the deal: I miss you, buddy.
His voice breaks.
The wives dab at their eyes. Bow their heads.
We pray.

All Da Single Ladies

By Mariam Williams

"I've been hoping for something different for you since you were eight months old."

I envision myself saying this to my cousin Mariah thirty years or so from now, when she is around my age and lets one of her innermost desires escape from her mouth. We're cheering a fictional couple's reunion on television, and in an unexpected moment of authenticity, she wonders aloud if singlehood is her destiny. I wonder when she learned other options exist.

When Mariah was eight months old, one of her aunts snapped a picture of her wearing a black sweater and eating cheese-stuffed pizza crust. Hot pink squiggly letters across the sweater read, "Single & Loving It!" Mariah's expression was that of a diva in the making: not a hint of a smile across her lips or in her dark brown eyes, her gaze daring someone to ask her for a bite. Her aunt put the picture on Facebook with the caption, "She ain't gotta share her pizza crust wit NOBODY!!! ALL DA SINGLE LADIES!"

Although I knew the baby's expression was luck and the caption was a joke, I couldn't help but think of the statistics and headlines inducing panic in black communities—"The

Erosion of the Black Family," "Seventy Percent of Black Children Raised by Single Moms," "Where Have All the Black Men Gone?"—and wonder if we were setting up Mariah to continue our family's manless, unmarried tradition.

Mariah's grandmother, my aunt, divorced several years before Mariah existed. Mariah's aunts, my first cousins, one seven years younger and the other seven years older than I, are single and have no shortage of admirers. Her twenty-two-year-old first cousin, my second cousin, lives with the boyfriend she chose over college. Mariah's mother, another one of my first cousins, has never been married, and wishes ill will upon the father of her first child. Mariah's brother is the only male in her daily life. From what I can tell—since my cousin doesn't share this information—Mariah sees her own father every other weekend, about as often she disappears from our neighborhood and returns with shirts boasting, "My Dad is Awesome."

My mother, Mariah's great-aunt, has never been married. My grandmother, Mariah's great-grandmother, was married for fifty-two years to a man our whole family loved deeply, but who died more than a decade before Mariah was born.

I fear Mariah will grow up witnessing a home life devoid of men as I simultaneously roll my eyes at the thought that this is something to be afraid of. An unplanned pregnancy at age thirty brought turbulence into my mother's life. Fights she had with her mother about having a child out of wedlock were legendary. She went on welfare just as Ronald Reagan was slashing federal budgets. She suffered jealousy of the latest woman my father never introduced as a girlfriend, abandonment by their mutual friends for becoming the responsible one as he remained the poet, and countless moments of awkwardness as she corrected my teachers and classmates' parents when they said, "Nice to meet you, Mrs. Williams," not considering she might be the single version of her maiden name.

But she saw to it that my life was good. I can't discredit my father—he was and remains an active co-parent whose devotion and presence were never lacking—but my mother maintained balance for me by keeping her family, which skews heavily female, nearby. From the day she brought me home from the hospital, we lived under the same roof with or in the same cozy neighborhood as her parents. The aunt and cousins that now form Mariah's network eventually replicated our living pattern. Screaming was frequent, but love was abundant.

At the academic and arts enrichment programs that filled my summers, I met wealthy white children angry over their parents' divorces. I hid my pride that my parents were smarter than theirs. I always attended excellent schools and graduated from one of the highest-ranked colleges in the country. I've never been pregnant. Aside from the embarrassment of living in my mother's house during a horrendous economy, I'm doing okay.

Except that I've been on three dates in the past two and a half years. My married friends and I rarely speak. I hear heartache on my behalf, through the phone no less, from the one friend who is single, but in a relationship headed toward marriage. I avoid my Sunday school class because it's full of happy couples, and attending is just another way to make myself feel excluded from the dating rituals normal twenty-

and thirty-somethings go through. Between age twenty-three, when I started dating, and my current age of thirty-one, I had two boyfriends. I have never brought anyone home to meet my family, I have no prospects, and seeing Mariah is the highlight of my week.

I shunned the thought of marriage and children for years and still question the benefits of domesticity for women. My mother never wanted to be a wife, and she lives by the motto, "I can do bad by myself." But bad alone isn't so good for me anymore. I have come to understand how the man of the house shaped the woman I am today. Had my grandfather not been the epitome of patience, wisdom, meekness, and peace in his household, I would not know humans could exhibit that kind of inner strength. He was the yang to a fiery, high-strung, estrogen-overloaded yin.

While I don't want to be bothered with men who don't embody my grandfather's qualities, the absence of romantic love—and, stronger yet, of inseparable-till-death love—was never my intent. I could choose the sacrificial love of a mother-child relationship on my own, but I know my life would have been different without witnessing my grandfather's commitment after fifty years of marriage, six children, nine grand- and great-grandchildren who turned his retirement years into parenthood, and another sixteen who didn't. He taught me that the man can be the one to give a seven-year-old a hug and ice cream after getting beat up by her cousins, that men still give anniversary flowers after forty years of marriage, that they can make excellent pancakes, and that having family around makes them happy. And when—if—I have children, I want them to see that.

I want Mariah to believe in the strength of women. I want her to retain her slight disdain for dresses and tights in favor of sweats and jeans she can crawl and roll around in. At eight months, she could bang her head on a piece of furniture she was trying to climb onto, take a tumble, and come right back up and try again, and I hope she never grows out of that. She is growing up at a time when, if I write, "John Doe and his wife, Jane," in a news story, I invariably get a note from my editor asking, "What is Jane's last name?" I ask business people I'm profiling *if* they have a spouse, fiancée, domestic partner, or significant other they'd like to mention. At the same time that some churches still see women as whores for having sex outside of marriage, "in a domestic partnership" is a choice for relationship status on Facebook. My cousin has choices, and she has expectations.

But I don't want others' expectations of what a woman's life should be, and of what a black woman's life will be, to limit her choices. I want Mariah to know the values of partnership and commitment, of expressions of love half a century into the game. She can take out her own trash and mow her lawn herself, just as all the women in her life do. She can hire a licensed mechanic, plumber, or electrician for anything she doesn't know how to do, just as any man who can't perform skilled labor would. But there's a different life out there, too, and I hope neither of us misses it.

Notes on Contest Winners

Eileen Malone's poetry has been published in more than 500 literary magazines and anthologies. Her collection of poetry *Letters with Taloned Claws* was published by Poets Corner Press and her book of poetry *I Should Have Given Them Water* was published by Ragged Sky Press. She founded and administers the Soul-Making Keats Literary Competition, now in its twentieth year. She lives in Broadmoor Village, California.

Caitlin O'Neil is a graduate of the MFA program at Columbia University and is currently a full-time lecturer in English at the University of Massachusetts Dartmouth. Her short fiction has appeared in the *Beloit Fiction Journal, Faultline, Drunken Boat,* and *Bridge Stories and Ideas,* and has been nominated for a Pushcart Prize. Her journalism has appeared in the *Boston Globe,* the *New York Times, Runners World, Budget Travel,* and *Poets and Writers*. She has been a resident at Community of Writers at Squaw Valley and the Vermont Studio Center.

Katie Caswell has had poetry selected for publication in *Kentucky Monthly*'s literary issue (November 2010) and the Louisville Eccentric Observer's *Literary LEO* (January 2008). In February 2011, her dramatic monologue, "Expectant Mother," was performed as a part of the BLOOM Theater Project in Louisville. In April 2011, her narrative "May 27th" was selected for *Kudzu* literary magazine. She teaches English at Assumption High School in Louisville where she enjoys sharing her passion for writing with her students.

Rachael Peckham's chapbook of prose poems, *Muck Fire* (Spring Garden Press) won the Robert Watson Poetry Award in 2010. Her poems and personal essays have appeared most recently in *Diagram, Edge, Gulf Coast, Sentence*, and *Under the Sun*. Currently, she is an assistant professor at Marshall University in Huntington, West Virginia, where she lives with her husband and son.

Andrea Bates is the author of the poetry chapbook *Origami Heart* (Toadlily Press); a poem from that collection was nominated for a Pushcart Prize. Her poetry is forthcoming in *Quiddity* and the twenty-fifth anniversary edition of *The Comstock Review*. Most recently, her poems have been published in *Inspired by Tagore*, an anthology published by the British Council; *200 New Mexico Poems; Tawdry Bawdry; The Evening Street Review;* and *Earth's Daughters*. She has won several awards for her work, including the Consequence Prize for a poem about war, and the California State Poetry Society's award for a poem about family, and she has twice won *The Lyricist* prize in its statewide competition. In 2012, the North Carolina Poetry Society awarded her work two first prizes in the Poetry of Courage and Poetry of Love Categories; and in 2011, she won the Society's Poet Laureate Award, and in 2010, the Thomas H. McDill Award. She teaches college writing and literature at Marine Corps Base Camp LeJeune and lives in Wilmington, North Carolina.

Jamie Hoey has been writing stories ever since she can remember. Her older sister read William Shakespeare's *Romeo and Juliet* aloud to her when she was four years old, and by age seven, she was reading Shakespeare on her own. Hoey is a recent graduate of Iowa State University's English literature program, and currently live in Des Moines with her husband and a dwarf bunny.

Ann Arbor, Michigan, is home for **Lakshmi Narayanan** and her husband, MP. A steady volunteer and an occasional writer, she draws much of her material from her childhood in India and her travels to India and other parts of the world.

Marina Petrova is a native of Moscow, Russia, but in the last fifteen years, she has lived in a small Tennessee town, Chicago and, finally, New York. She works in the field of media technology, but her passion is writing, reading, and finding a bit of alternate reality in the written word on the daily basis. She currently lives in New York City with her husband and son.

Notes on Member Contributors

Emily Boone is a licensed clinical social worker in private practice since 1979. She brings a rich, varied, and skilled background of experiences to each situation. She adventures into writing to share her intensity, insights, and stream-of-consciousness approaches through written media. Boone invites you to read her works and join her on these journeys of self-discovery and exploration. Her work has appeared in the 2011, 2010, and 2009 *Calliope* anthologies.

Cynthia Canada has been telling stories all her life; her first "book" was one she dictated to her mother when she was four years old and illustrated with her crayons and imagination. (She doesn't remember what it was about, but it almost certainly involved her imaginary friend, Manny Lee.) Decades later, she is a technical writer (it pays the bills), freelance journalist, and author of fiction and a smattering of poetry. She is a member of Women Who Write, the Freelancers' Union, and The Writers' Workshop of Asheville.

J. Watson Finger is a former educator and University of Louisville instructor, and has worked for the *Washington Post* and the *New York Times*. She has had articles published in *University of Louisville* magazine and the *Louisville Defender* newspaper, and has presented workshops at the University of Louisville. She is a current member of the National Trust for Historic Preservation and the Kentucky Historical Society, and has participated as a Diversity Scholar. She is also a visual artist and has exhibited with the Ky African American organization throughout the tri-state area. Finger also appears as a member of the Montage artists' organization in *Two Centuries of Black Louisville*. She is presently working on a children's novel and anthology.

Margaret Grimes was born in West Virginia, educated there and in Ohio. Early in her married life, she moved to Louisville, Kentucky, where she still resides. She has been a language teacher, a school director, a marketing promotions manager, and a development officer. Language and writing have been her passion all her life. Now retired, she enjoys the writing community of Louisville. She is currently associate director of Women Who Write, Inc. Grimes has been published in marketing communications, and in the 2010 *Calliope, Home for the Holidays: Stories and Recipes,* and *Cooking Comfort: Stories and Recipes*. She also contributed to *Keeneland Entertains,* a special publication by the Keeneland Association, celebrating the 75th anniversary of the Keeneland Racetrack. She is about to publish a memoir of childhood stories.

Carroll Grossman is a teacher, speech-language pathologist, and writer who lives and works in Louisville, Kentucky. She was born and raised in the mountains of eastern Kentucky, and the many hours spent wandering among the hills and creeks there left an enduring love of the outdoors and a passion for preserving the beauty and natural resources in Kentucky. Many of her stories and poems reflect the honest, strong, and complex character of those living in economic poverty surrounded by mountains big enough to slow the sunrise. Grossman was the third-place poetry winner in the 2011 Women Who Write prose and poetry contest, and has since joined the organization. Her work has been published in *Edible Louisville*, the 2011 *Calliope*, and in an anthology used in writing classes at a local college. She is a founding member of the Cherokee Roundtable, a group of local writers.

Susan E. Lindsey is a writer, book editor, and newspaper columnist. Her work has been published in *Underwired*, the 2011 *Calliope* and other anthologies, *The Highlander*, on RaphaelsVillage.com, and in corporate publications. She has won or placed in several writing competitions. Lindsey worked in corporate communication and public relations for nearly twenty years before launching her own company, Savvy Communication LLC (www.savvy-comm.com). She is director of Women Who Write, and a member of the American Copy Editors Society, the Editorial Freelancers Association, the Talking Story writers' group, and numerous historical and genealogical societies.

Mariam Williams is a widely published freelance journalist and a writer recognized by media and arts institutions for excellence in journalism, creative nonfiction, copywriting, and script writing. Her accolades include awards in first and third place in 2011 and 2012, respectively, for Best Column Writing from the Louisville Chapter of the Society of Professional Journalists, an Al J. Smith Emerging Artist Award from the Kentucky Arts Council, the Gabehart Prize from the Kentucky Women Writers Conference, two Artist Enrichment grants from the Kentucky Foundation for Women, and a Juneteenth Festival Playwriting Award from University of Louisville. Since 2009, Williams has worked as a featured columnist for the *Courier-Journal*. She is a regular contributor to *Underwired* magazine and has been published in *Business First, The Lane Report,* and on EBONY.com. Ms. Williams holds a bachelor's degree from Washington University in St. Louis and a certificate in screenwriting from the University of California Los Angeles.

Books Available from Women Who Write

Women Who Write, Inc. is a 501(c)(3) organization. Donations are gratefully accepted to support the group's mission and are tax-deductible. The following books are publications of Women Who Write, and are available on Amazon.com or can be ordered from the Women Who Write website: www.womenwhowrite.com or ordered by mail (see order form on next page).

Calliope: The 19th Annual Anthology (2012)
Calliope: The 18th Annual Anthology (2011)
Calliope: The 17th Annual Anthology (2010)
Calliope: The 16th Annual Anthology (2009)
Home for the Holidays: Stories and Recipes (2011)
Comfort Cooking: Stories with Recipes (2010)

Order Form

Please send me _____ copies of *Calliope, the 19th Annual Anthology of Women Who Write* at $12 each, plus $3 each for shipping and handling. I have enclosed a check payable to Women Who Write for the total of $_______.

Mail order and check to:
Women Who Write
P.O. Box 6167
Louisville, KY 40206-0167

Ship books to:
Name ____
Address ______________________________________
City _______________________ ST ____ Zip _______
Daytime phone (____) ______-_______
Email address __________________________________

Questions? Email us at info@womenwhowrite.com or director@womenwhowrite.com.

www.ingramcontent.com/pod-product-compliance
Lightning Source LLC
LaVergne TN
LVHW010931110826
845149LV00013B/2547

* 9 7 8 0 9 8 8 3 6 7 3 0 2 *